# Excel
## Get the Results You Want!

# Year 3
# Thinking Skills
# Tests

**Sharon Dalgleish,
Tanya Dalgleish
& Hamish McLean**

PASCAL
PRESS

© 2023 Sharon Dalgleish, Tanya Dalgleish, Hamish McLean and Pascal Press

**Completely new edition incorporating 2021 Opportunity Class Test changes**

Reprinted 2024

ISBN 978 1 74125 700 7

Pascal Press Pty Ltd
PO Box 250
Glebe NSW 2037
(02) 9198 1748
www.pascalpress.com.au

Publisher: Vivienne Joannou
Project editor: Mark Dixon
Edited by Mark Dixon and Rosemary Peers
Answers checked by Dale Little and Peter Little
Cover by DiZign Pty Ltd
Typeset by Grizzly Graphics (Leanne Richters)
Printed by Vivar Printing/Green Giant Press

# Contents

**Introduction**................................................................................................................**iv**
About this book.................................................................................................................iv
About the Opportunity Class Test..................................................................................iv
Advice to students..............................................................................................................v
**Sample answer sheet**................................................................................................**vi**

## Test skill explanation and practice pages

Identifying the main idea.................................................................................................1
Identifying a conclusion that must be true..................................................................2
Identifying a conclusion that is not possible...............................................................3
Identifying evidence that leads to a conclusion.........................................................4
Identifying an assumption................................................................................................5
Identifying correct reasoning..........................................................................................6
Identifying flawed reasoning...........................................................................................8
Identifying additional evidence to strengthen a claim.............................................9
Identifying additional evidence to weaken an argument......................................10
Sharing items out evenly...............................................................................................11
Calculations involving time...........................................................................................12
Using a process of elimination.....................................................................................13
Finding hidden information...........................................................................................14
Solving 3D puzzles...........................................................................................................15
Viewing objects from different sides...........................................................................17
Reading timetables.........................................................................................................19
Questions about graphs.................................................................................................21
Identifying and following a pattern.............................................................................22

## Sample tests

Sample Test 1A.................................................................................................................23
Sample Test 1B.................................................................................................................27
Sample Test 2A.................................................................................................................30
Sample Test 2B.................................................................................................................34
Sample Test 3A.................................................................................................................38
Sample Test 3B.................................................................................................................42
Sample Test 4A.................................................................................................................46
Sample Test 4B.................................................................................................................50
Sample Test 5A.................................................................................................................54
Sample Test 5B.................................................................................................................58

## Answers

Practice questions............................................................................................................61
Sample tests......................................................................................................................67

# INTRODUCTION

## ABOUT THIS BOOK

This book has been written to help develop students' thinking skills. Thinking skills involve two disciplines: critical thinking and problem solving.

**Critical thinking** means the ability to analyse a claim or argument; identify whether it is flawed or uses correct reasoning; and determine whether the evidence, assumptions and conclusion are warranted.

**Problem solving** as a thinking skill means the ability to use numerical or mathematical skills to work out solutions to problems. These include visualising and rotating solids in three-dimensional space; ordering a number of objects based on comparisons and characteristics; analysing graphs and diagrams; and solving mathematical puzzles involving numbers, shapes and time.

In the Australian Curriculum both critical and creative thinking are described as important skills in all the eight key learning areas: English, mathematics, science, humanities and social sciences, the arts, technologies, health and physical education, and languages.

Critical-thinking and problem-solving skills are also valuable in everyday life as well as in many fields of endeavour students might eventually embark upon.

The first section of this book teaches students 18 thinking skills. Each thinking skill is first defined, then a sample question is provided and the solution is worked through for the student as a teaching/learning exercise. Then two practice questions are provided. These are for the student to attempt independently. The solutions are worked through in the answer section of the book.

This section is followed by ten practice tests comprising 15 questions each. Each test includes an equal mixture of critical-thinking and problem-solving questions.

Answers and detailed explanations are provided at the back of the book. Most answers include the working out.

If you would like to use this book to help you prepare specifically for the Opportunity Class Test, you can merge two Sample Tests and have your child complete the two tests in 30 minutes.

One test will therefore comprise 30 questions, which is equivalent to the length of the Thinking Skills paper in the NSW Opportunity Class Placement Test. For example, you could merge Sample Test 1A with Sample Test 1B to form Test 1.

## ABOUT THE OPPORTUNITY CLASS TEST

This book is excellent preparation for the Thinking Skills section of the NSW Opportunity Class Placement Test, which is taken by students in Year 4.

The NSW Opportunity Class Placement Test is required for placement in an Opportunity Class in a NSW public school.

This type of class offers an extra challenge for academically gifted students with high potential in Years 5 and 6. Selection is based on academic merit.

Details are available at: https://education.nsw.gov.au.

The tests were updated in 2021 with a greater emphasis on literacy, thinking skills, mathematical reasoning and problem solving. The General Ability Test has been replaced by a Thinking Skills Test. The new NSW Opportunity Class Placement Test adjusts and balances the weighting given to the Reading, Thinking Skills and Mathematical Reasoning components. These changes were in response to the findings of the 2018 Review of Selective Education Access report, commissioned by the NSW Department of Education.

The NSW Opportunity Class Placement Test consists of three multiple-choice sections:

- **Reading** (25 questions in 30 minutes)
- **Mathematical Reasoning** (35 questions in 40 minutes)
- **Thinking Skills** (30 questions in 30 minutes).

## ADVICE TO STUDENTS

Each question in the NSW Opportunity Class Placement Test is multiple choice. This means you have to choose the correct answer from the given options.

We have included a sample answer sheet in this book for you to practise on. Note that from 2025, however, the NSW Opportunity Class Placement Test will change to a computer-based test.

Some of the more challenging Thinking Skills problem-solving questions could take you up to 10 minutes to complete to begin with, as you may use diagrams or tables to help you solve them. Remember that the more questions you do of this same type, the faster you will become— until you know exactly how to solve them.

# Thinking Skills sample answer sheet

Mark your answers here.

To answer each question, fill in the appropriate circle for your chosen answer.

Use a pencil. If you make a mistake or change your mind, erase and try again.

You can make extra copies of this answer sheet to mark your answers to all the Sample Tests in this book.

## Test A

| | A B C D | | A B C D | | A B C D | | A B C D |
|---|---|---|---|---|---|---|---|
| 1 | ○○○○ | 6 | ○○○○ | 11 | ○○○○ | 16 | ○○○○ |
| 2 | ○○○○ | 7 | ○○○○ | 12 | ○○○○ | 17 | ○○○○ |
| 3 | ○○○○ | 8 | ○○○○ | 13 | ○○○○ | 18 | ○○○○ |
| 4 | ○○○○ | 9 | ○○○○ | 14 | ○○○○ | 19 | ○○○○ |
| 5 | ○○○○ | 10 | ○○○○ | 15 | ○○○○ | 20 | ○○○○ |

## Test B

| | A B C D | | A B C D | | A B C D | | A B C D |
|---|---|---|---|---|---|---|---|
| 1 | ○○○○ | 6 | ○○○○ | 11 | ○○○○ | 16 | ○○○○ |
| 2 | ○○○○ | 7 | ○○○○ | 12 | ○○○○ | 17 | ○○○○ |
| 3 | ○○○○ | 8 | ○○○○ | 13 | ○○○○ | 18 | ○○○○ |
| 4 | ○○○○ | 9 | ○○○○ | 14 | ○○○○ | 19 | ○○○○ |
| 5 | ○○○○ | 10 | ○○○○ | 15 | ○○○○ | 20 | ○○○○ |

## Identifying the main idea

- The main idea is the idea or conclusion the creator of the text wants you to accept is true. It's often stated at the beginning of a text but could also be at the end or anywhere else in the text. The rest of the text will support or add to, or give you reasons to believe, this main idea.

- Read the question text carefully and think about what the creator of the text wants you to accept. Underline the sentence you think could be the main idea. Check to see if the rest of the text gives you reasons to believe this main idea. Read each answer option in turn to evaluate if it expresses the main idea. Quickly eliminate any answers that are definitely wrong.

### SAMPLE QUESTION

In the wild, animals choose their own meals but in a zoo the meals of the animals are carefully planned by zoo nutritionists. They try to give each animal the same kinds of food it would have in the wild. Or they find other foods that are good for the animal. Zoo nutritionists also figure out how much food each animal should have. It's a job for a specialist!

Which statement best expresses the main idea of the text?

A  Animals choose their own meals in the wild.

B  Different meal plans are made for baby and adult animals.

C  Zoo nutritionists plan the meals of zoo animals.

D  Zoo nutritionists figure out how much food an animal should have.

**C is correct. The main idea the creator of the text wants you to accept is that zoo nutritionists plan the meals of zoo animals. The rest of the text supports this main idea by giving more information about what zoo nutritionists do. The final sentence also reinforces the main idea.**

**A is incorrect.** This idea is mentioned in the opening sentence but the creator of the text has used it as a hook to introduce the text. It is not the main idea the creator of the text wants you to accept.

**B is incorrect.** This information is not in the text so cannot be the main idea.

**D is incorrect.** This is supporting information for the main idea.

###  Practice questions

**1** Good news! Greenhill Botanic Gardens is now open for visitors after the damage caused by the windstorm before Christmas. Take a walk along our paths, have a picnic, sit by the pond or have fun in the children's areas. Our nursery is also open with plenty of native plants on sale. They are all ready for planting once the weather cools.

Which statement best expresses the main idea of the text?

A  Greenhill Botanic Gardens were damaged by a windstorm.

B  Greenhill Botanic Gardens are now open.

C  Volunteers run the Greenhill Botanic Gardens nursery.

D  Greenhill Botanic Gardens has paths, picnic areas and a pond.

**2** Cats are afraid of cucumbers! The shape of a cucumber resembles a snake and cats are not fond of snakes. Even if a cat has never seen a snake in its life, cats are naturally hardwired to consider snakes a threat. So any object that suddenly appears and resembles a snake can scare a cat. That includes cucumbers!

Which statement best expresses the main idea of the text?

A  Cats are afraid of cucumbers.

B  The shape of a cucumber resembles a snake.

C  Cats can eat cucumbers cut into bite-sized pieces.

D  Cats never see snakes in real life.

# Identifying a conclusion that must be true

- To draw a conclusion you need to read and assess all the information and evidence provided. A conclusion can only be true if it is supported by evidence. A conclusion can be eliminated if there is evidence that contradicts it, or if there is no evidence or incomplete evidence to support it.
- Read the question carefully. Judge which conclusion must be true based on the evidence in the text. As you read the answer options, try to quickly eliminate any conclusion that has evidence to contradict it. Also eliminate any conclusion that is neither proved nor disproved because the evidence is incomplete or unavailable.

## SAMPLE QUESTION

Clara, Bree, Cooper and Felix are all friends with Alice.

**Alice:** 'Mum says we can't all fit in the car to go to the movies on the weekend. So if Clara can't come, then I'll ask Bree to come. But if Clara can come, then I'll ask Cooper instead of Felix.'

If Alice does not ask Bree to the movies, which of the other three does she ask?

A Clara and Cooper
B Cooper and Felix
C Clara only
D Felix only

**A is correct.** If Alice did not ask Bree to the movies, you can conclude that Clara must be able to come. Since Clara is able to come, then Alice must also ask Cooper.

**B is incorrect.** Alice says she will ask Cooper or Felix, not both.

**C is incorrect.** Alice says if she asks Clara, she will also ask Cooper.

**D is incorrect.** We know that since Alice did not ask Bree then Clara must be able to come, so Alice must ask Cooper instead of Felix.

## Practice questions

**1** Arlo's class was participating in a readathon. Mr Lin told the class: 'To have even a chance of receiving a prize in the readathon you must have read at least 20 books.'

If Mr Lin is correct, which of these statements will be true?
A All the students who have read 20 books will receive a prize.
B Only the students who have read less than 20 books will receive a prize.
C None of the students who have read less than 20 books will receive a prize.
D Some of the students who have read less than 20 books will receive a prize.

**2** Grandma, Dad and Isla are planning what to do in the holidays. Grandma says she wants to go on a picnic, ride a motor bike, do some gardening, go bushwalking and go to the beach. Dad says he wants to visit Uncle Frank, go to the beach and play golf. Isla wants to go on a picnic, have a sleepover, go bushwalking, play golf and see a movie.

Which activities does Grandma want to do that neither Dad nor Isla wants to do?
A picnic and ride a motorbike
B gardening and bushwalking
C golf and visit Uncle Frank
D ride a motorbike and garden

## Identifying a conclusion that is not possible

- To be able to draw a conclusion you need to consider all the evidence. For a conclusion to be true or correct it has to be supported by evidence. You can work out when a conclusion is not possible or cannot be true because there won't be evidence to support it.
- Read the question carefully. When working out your answer you should try to quickly eliminate any options that are obviously incorrect. These will be the conclusions that are true. This will narrow down your choice.
- Judge which conclusion cannot be true by deciding that there is no evidence to support it.

### SAMPLE QUESTION

Band practice is held twice a week after school but never two days in a row. An extra practice is often also called before school when needed.

Which one of the statements below **cannot** be true?

A This week practices will be held on Monday and Wednesday afternoons and on Friday morning.

B This week practices will be held on Wednesday and Friday afternoons.

C This week practices will be held on Tuesday morning and on Thursday and Friday afternoons.

D This week practices will be held on Monday and Friday afternoons and on Wednesday morning.

**C is correct. It cannot be true that practices will be held on Thursday and Friday afternoons. The information tells you practices are never held two days in a row.**

**A is incorrect.** This statement could be true because Monday, Wednesday and Friday are not two days in a row.

**B is incorrect.** This statement could be true because Wednesday and Friday are not two days in a row.

**D is incorrect.** Practice sessions could be held on Monday and Friday afternoons and on Wednesday morning. These practices are not two days in a row.

 **Practice questions**

**1** Jeannie walks to school with her friends Adam and Lana except on Tuesdays when she has swimming before school. On that day her father drives her.

Which sentence below **cannot** be true?

A Jeannie walked to school on Monday with Adam and Lana.

B Adam and Lana walked to school on Tuesday without Jeannie.

C On Tuesday Jeannie had swimming practice so did not go to school by car.

D On Friday Jeannie went to school on foot.

**2** Colin plans to buy a guitar.

- There is an offer available from one music store where he can buy a guitar and get a hard case for it for free.
- Another store is offering five free guitar lessons with every guitar purchased.
- The guitar Colin wants is the same price at each store above but he has to wait a month for stock to arrive.
- A third store has stock and the guitar is the same price but there's no free case or music lessons.

If all the above statements are true, only one of the sentences below **cannot** be true. Which one?

A Colin purchased a guitar and got five free lessons but had to wait a month to receive his guitar.

B Colin decided not to buy a new guitar after all.

C Colin purchased a guitar and got it immediately but did not get a case for it.

D Colin purchased a guitar with a free case and took it home immediately.

# Identifying evidence that leads to a conclusion

- To draw a conclusion you need evidence that supports the conclusion. Sometimes you can't work out a conclusion because there is not enough evidence.
- It is important to be able to judge whether or not evidence directly leads to a conclusion.
- These types of questions are not asking you to draw a conclusion but instead to judge which option helps you to know the conclusion.
- You need to eliminate the options that won't lead to a conclusion or that don't help you work out the conclusion.

## SAMPLE QUESTION

Ted's T-ball team needed to decide on a new team name. They had narrowed their choices down to three: Sluggers, Gorillas or Raptors. They decided to have a vote. Every team member got two votes but could not use both votes on the same team name. The name would only be changed if everyone voted for it with one of their votes. Every team name got at least one vote.

Knowing **one** of the following would allow you to know the result of the vote. Which one is it?

A   Every student voted for either Gorillas or Raptors, or both.

B   Sluggers was one of the two more popular names.

C   No-one voted for both Sluggers and Gorillas.

D   Only two people voted for Gorillas.

**C is correct. All five people had two votes each. Knowing that no-one voted for both Sluggers and Gorillas tells you that everyone voted for Raptors; that is, they must have voted for either Sluggers and Raptors with their two votes or Gorillas and Raptors.**

**A is incorrect.** This information does not allow you to know the result of the vote.

**B is incorrect.** This information does not allow you to know the result of the vote. It only narrows the choice to two: Sluggers and one other.

**D is incorrect.** This information does not allow you to know the result of the vote. It only tells you that Gorillas did not win the vote.

## Practice questions

1   There are eight people in our extended family. Mum gave everyone in the family two pieces of paper and told them to write their two top choices for takeaway dinner on Saturday night. The choices were Japanese, Thai or Chinese food. She said they each had to write two different choices on their papers. Every food got at least one vote.

Knowing **one** of the following allows you to know what food the family had on Saturday night. Which one?

A   Thai received three votes.

B   Japanese was one of the more popular votes.

C   Every one voted for either Thai or Chinese, or both.

D   No-one voted for both Japanese and Thai.

2   One of the stalls for the school fete planned to serve healthy smoothies on fete day. Year 3 was running the stall and needed to decide on a name for their stall. The class liked Sweet Tooth Smoothies, Smoothie Paradise and Secret Garden Smoothies. Everyone in the class got to vote for their two favourite names. Every name got at least ten votes.

Knowing **one** of the following allows you to know the result of the vote. Which one?

A   Everyone voted for either Smoothie Paradise or Secret Garden Smoothies, or both.

B   Sweet Tooth Smoothies was one of the two top votes.

C   No student voted for both Sweet Tooth Smoothies and Smoothie Paradise.

D   Smoothie Paradise received ten votes.

## Identifying an assumption

- An assumption is not stated in a text. It is something missing that has been assumed or taken for granted to draw a conclusion. An assumption is not necessarily true but the person making the assumption believes it is. (For this reason, making assumptions can lead to incorrect conclusions!)
- To identify an assumption, you first have to read the text carefully and identify the conclusion that has been made. Then identify the evidence on which that conclusion is based. Finally, read and think about each answer option listed. These are the possible assumptions. Which one of those options would you need to take for granted to draw the conclusion from the evidence in the text? You can think about it like this:

evidence + the missing assumption = conclusion.

### SAMPLE QUESTION

Each student in Harper's class must prepare and give a presentation on a topic of their own choice.

**Harper:** 'I'm going to do my presentation on spiders.'
**Kale:** 'You must really like spiders!'
**Harper:** 'No, I don't. But my aunt has a pet tarantula I could bring in.'

Which assumption has Kale made to draw his conclusion?

A  Harper really likes spiders.
B  Harper's aunt has a pet tarantula.
C  Harper chose spiders for her presentation topic.
D  Students only choose topics that they really like.

**D is correct.** Kale's conclusion is that Harper really likes spiders. He based this conclusion on the evidence that Harper chose spiders for her presentation topic. So, for his conclusion to hold, it must be assumed that students only choose topics they really like. (Harper chose spiders for her presentation topic + students only choose topics they really like means therefore Harper really likes spiders.) Harper goes on to tell Kale

that she does not like spiders. So, in this instance, Kale's assumption led him to an incorrect conclusion.

**A is incorrect.** This is Kale's conclusion, not his assumption.

**B is incorrect.** This is the real reason why Harper chooses spiders for her presentation topic. However, it is not the assumption Kale has made and it **does not** lead to the conclusion Kale came to. (Harper chooses spiders for her presentation topic + Harper's aunt has a pet tarantula **does not** mean therefore Harper really likes spiders.)

**C is incorrect.** This is the evidence Kale has used to draw his conclusion.

###  Practice questions

1. A local store displayed a sign on the counter:

The Council wants to build a new car park.
We must support the idea!
Sign the petition here!

Which assumption has the writer of the sign made?
A  The Council wants to build a new car park.
B  Building a new car park is a good thing.
C  We must support the idea to build a new car park.
D  We should not build a new car park.

2. Harvey and Violet are best friends. They are waiting in line to ride the roller-coaster.

**Harvey:** 'It's scarier at the front of the cars.'
**Violet:** 'Okay, we'll sit up front then.'

Which assumption has Violet made to draw her conclusion?
A  Harvey wants to be scared.
B  Harvey does not like being scared.
C  They should sit up front.
D  It's scarier at the front of the cars.

# Identifying correct reasoning

- When someone makes a claim or presents their point of view they use reasoning to support their claim. Their reasoning must make sense and be based on the facts available.
- When you read or listen to a claim you need to analyse the reasoning. If the reasoning is correct, you might accept the claim. If the reasoning does not make sense or is mistaken, you can reject the claim.
- These kinds of questions ask you to judge if the reasoning is correct. Read the question carefully. When working out your answer, eliminate answers that are incorrect until you find the answer that is correct.

## SAMPLE QUESTION

Li Mei wants to go to the Royal Easter Show on the weekend. To be allowed to go she knows that she has to make her parents happy. She will definitely make her parents happy if she gets a good mark in her spelling test on Friday and if she helps all week with the household chores.

**Ava:** 'If Li Mei goes to the Royal Easter Show, she must have got a good mark in her spelling test on Friday and helped with the household chores all week.'

**Lewis:** 'If Li Mei doesn't go to the Royal Easter Show, she can't have got a good mark in her spelling test on Friday or helped with the household chores.'

If the information in the box is true, whose reasoning is correct?

A  Ava only
B  Lewis only
C  Both Ava and Lewis
D  Neither Ava nor Lewis

**D is correct. Neither Ava nor Lewis uses correct reasoning.**

**A is incorrect.** Ava can't be certain that if Li Mei goes to the Royal Easter Show, she must have got a good mark in her spelling test on Friday and helped with the household chores all week. Li Mei had to make her parents happy to be allowed to go to the Royal Easter Show. Ava's reasoning is incorrect. There may be other ways for Li Mei to make her parents happy.

**B is incorrect.** Lewis cannot reason that if Li Mei does not go to the Royal Easter Show, it's because she can't have got a good mark in her spelling test on Friday and helped with the household chores. There may be other reasons for Li Mei not making her parents happy. Lewis's reasoning is incorrect.

**C is incorrect** by a process of elimination.

 **Practice questions**

**1** Due to the pandemic, only those aged-care residents who have a family member to sign them out and vouch for their safety will be allowed out of the facility this weekend, providing there are no further government lockdowns.

**Lina:** 'Eric does not have a family member to sign him out so he definitely won't be allowed out of the facility this weekend.'

**Simon:** 'Pauline has a family member coming to sign her out and vouch for her safety so she will be allowed out of the facility this weekend.'

## Identifying correct reasoning

If the information in the box is true, whose reasoning is correct?

A   Lina only

B   Simon only

C   Both Lina and Simon

D   Neither Lina nor Simon

 **2**

The alarm starts to beep when the battery is running low on charge. This beeping will continue for 24 hours. The lower the charge, the louder the beep until there's an alarm and then ten minutes later the battery will be dead and the beeping will stop.

**Brooke**: 'Because the beep tells when the battery is running low it's also useful to tell when the battery still has a charge because the battery won't have been beeping.'

**Amy:** 'If the battery isn't beeping, there's no need to replace it.'

If the information in the box is true, whose reasoning is correct?

A   Brooke only

B   Amy only

C   Both Brooke and Amy

D   Neither Brooke nor Amy

# Identifying flawed reasoning

- When someone makes a claim, they use reasoning to support that claim. Their reasoning must make sense and be based on the facts available.
- When you read or listen to a claim you need to analyse the reasoning. If the reasoning does not make sense or the person making the claim has made a mistake, then you can reject their claim or conclusion.
- These kinds of questions ask you to identify if someone has made a mistake in their reasoning. Read the question carefully. When working out your answer, quickly eliminate options that are obviously incorrect until you find the one that is correct—the one with flawed reasoning.

## SAMPLE QUESTION

**Bradley:** 'If you hope to get selected for the volleyball team. you need to have attended at least two of the six practice sessions offered during the week.'

**Alexandria:** 'I attended two of the practice sessions so I am sure to get selected for the team.'

If what Bradley says is true, which of the following shows Alexandria's mistake?

A  Many players want to be selected for the team.

B  Practice sessions are not as important as having a positive attitude.

C  Practising for the minimum only gives you hope of being selected.

D  Volleyball is a fun team game.

**C is correct. Bradley has advised that Alexandria needs to have attended at least two of the six practice sessions offered during the week if she hopes to get selected for the volleyball team. Alexandria has incorrectly reasoned that she only needs to attend two and she will be sure to get selected. The minimum amount of practice might not be enough.**

**A is incorrect.** The statement that many players want to be selected for the team might be true but this is not the mistake in reasoning made by Alexandria.

**B is incorrect.** This statement is unlikely to be true given the importance of attending practice sessions but it is also not the mistake made by Alexandria.

**D is incorrect.** This statement might be true but it is not the error in reasoning that Alexandria made.

## Practice questions

 1  Elsa and Lachlan are in a grocery store.

**Elsa:** 'Nana says she wants a pack of the plain biscuits that come in red wrapping. She can't remember the brand but they are her favourite biscuits.'

**Lachlan:** 'Here's a pack of plain biscuits. The wrapping's brown, not red, but there are no other packs here so this must be the one she wants. Nana must have made a mistake with the colour.'

Which one of the following shows the mistake Lachlan has made?

A  Because he can't find plain biscuits in a red wrapper he thinks Nana has made a mistake.

B  He thinks Elsa has forgotten the brand.

C  As long as they buy plain biscuits it doesn't matter what brand they are.

D  Elsa and Lachlan are looking in the wrong store.

 2

**Mr Dreyfus:** 'My class is hosting a Grandparents' Day this Friday. Only twelve children have responded that their grandparents will be coming. The rest of the children must not have living grandparents.'

Which one of the following is the mistake that Mr Dreyfus has made?

A  He did not invite grandparents from other classes.

B  He did not identify which children had grandparents attending.

C  Some of the children in the class might have grandparents who live too far away to attend.

D  He thinks that every grandparent will attend Grandparents' Day.

## Identifying additional evidence to strengthen a claim

- An argument presents someone's point of view or makes a claim. It uses evidence to convince others to accept this point of view or claim. An argument can be supported or strengthened with further evidence or extra information.
- To identify the statement that best supports or most strengthens an argument or claim, read the text carefully. Identify the argument or claim being made in the text then consider the answer options listed. Assess the impact of each one on the argument you identified. Look for the option that gives further evidence to support the argument or claim, or that most strengthens it. Try to quickly eliminate any answers that are definitely incorrect or irrelevant to the argument.

### SAMPLE QUESTION

**Taj:** 'Let's go to the movies on Saturday. I really want to see that new movie!'

**Ava:** 'We should do a walking tour of Headland Reserve this Saturday and see the movie next week. The tour guide points out all the unique animals and plants. We don't want to miss out. We might see an echidna or even an eagle soaring above.'

Which one of these statements, if true, best supports Ava's claim?

A   The Headland Reserve walking tour is only held this Saturday.

B   The weather forecast is for rain on Saturday.

C   Headland Reserve has many unique plants and animals.

D   Headland Reserve is close to where both Taj and Ava live.

**A is correct. Ava claims they should go on the walking tour this Saturday and see the movie next week. She supports this by saying they don't want to miss out on seeing the plants and animals. The statement that the tour is only held this Saturday best supports this, since if they don't go this Saturday they will miss out.**

**B is incorrect.** This statement could support an argument to go to the movies instead, so it does not best support Ava's claim.

**C is incorrect.** Ava has already mentioned that there are unique plants and animals so this statement does not add anything new to support her claim.

**D is incorrect.** This statement is not relevant to the claim that they should go to the Reserve this Saturday and then the movies next Saturday.

### Practice questions

1. The local council is urging the community to remain vigilant about mosquitoes. The council says that some mosquitoes can transmit serious diseases. They are reminding people to reduce the risk of mosquitoes breeding by cleaning up around the yard to remove or empty anything that holds water.

   Which one of these statements, if true, best supports the council's claim?

   A   The word mosquito is Spanish for 'little fly'.

   B   Mosquitoes can be a nuisance.

   C   Mosquitoes use six needles when they suck your blood.

   D   Surveillance trappings show that mosquito numbers are higher than usual.

2. A volunteer from a therapy dog organisation said in a television interview: 'Having a bond with animals improves the quality of life for humans. Attention from a dog has been scientifically proven to improve overall health and wellbeing.'

   Which one of these statements, if true, best supports the volunteer's claim?

   A   Pet dogs can be assessed as therapy dogs.

   B   Therapy dogs work in hospitals, aged-care facilities and other community services.

   C   Research shows that stroking a dog can lower blood pressure and ease feelings of anxiety.

   D   The therapy dog organisation is fundraising to train more dogs and volunteers.

☞ Answers and explanations on page 63

# Identifying additional evidence to weaken an argument

- When someone makes a claim or presents a point of view or an argument, they provide reasons to support their claim.
- Any statement that calls into question or contradicts any of the evidence for the claim will weaken the claim.
- Look for the following:
  - a statement that contradicts evidence in the claim
  - a statement that undermines the accuracy of the claim
  - a statement that limits the scope of the claim
  - any statement that makes the claim less likely to hold up.

Read the questions below carefully. When working out your answers, eliminate any that are incorrect until you find the answer that is correct.

## SAMPLE QUESTION

Ken is trying to lose weight and claims that having precooked meals delivered to his home reduces his chances of overeating and supports his efforts to lose weight.

Which statement **weakens** Ken's claim above?

A There is a pizza restaurant near Ken's home that has been delivering to Ken's regularly.

B Not all food deliveries arrive on time.

C Ken plans to order healthy meal options.

D The precooked meals might not all be healthy.

**D is correct. Ken's claim is that having precooked meals delivered to his home will make it easier for him to lose weight. The issue that the precooked meals might not all be healthy weakens Ken's claim.**

**A is incorrect.** The statement that there is a pizza restaurant near Ken's home that has been delivering to Ken's regularly is irrelevant to the claim. Also you can assume that Ken will not order pizza once he starts ordering precooked meals to lose weight.

**B is incorrect.** The statement that not all food deliveries arrive on time is irrelevant to the claim about whether the precooked meals will help Ken lose weight.

**C is incorrect.** The fact that Ken plans to order healthy meal options strengthens his claim. Also you can assume that Ken will try to order healthy options if his goal is to lose weight.

## Practice questions

1 More children at the school prefer attending the swimming carnival to the athletics carnival because of the weather. The swimming carnival is usually held in March when it's still warm enough to enjoy being in the pool. The athletics carnival is usually held in August, which is known to be a windy time of year and therefore being a spectator is unpleasant.

Which statement **weakens** the above argument?

A Sometimes the swimming carnival is held in the cooler month of April.

B Last year the swimming carnival was held in February.

C Children are advised to bring warm clothes to the athletics carnival.

D All children are encouraged to participate in the carnivals.

2 **Bruno:** 'The gym in our building is mainly used by residents aged over 65 who have retired from work and have time to visit the gym. Many more of our residents are expected to reach the age of 65 over the next five years so we anticipate that the gym will become busier.'

Which statement **weakens** the above claim?

A People who retire from work like to keep fit.

B There is a trend for people to continue working past the age of 65.

C Extra equipment will be needed when the gym becomes busier.

D 65-year-olds today are healthier than 65-year-olds in the past.

    ☞ Answers and explanations on pages 63–64

## Sharing items out evenly

- When a question asks you to share things between people or piles, knowing your times tables becomes very important. If you don't know them that well, you can draw the things on paper in equal piles to work out the answer.
- Some questions use words like **must** and **certain**. Some questions use words like **at least** or **at most**.
- A question that asks whether something **must be true** does not mean the same as a question that asks whether something **can be true**.
- For example, if you flip a coin, it **can be true** that it will show a tail. This does not mean that it must be true. We know that it is also possible to get a head.
- The question below asks how many piles **must** have **at least** one white card. So you need to work out what is the smallest number of piles possible with white cards.

### SAMPLE QUESTION

Vivian deals 15 cards into five piles so that each pile has the same number of cards. There are two red cards, five black cards, and the rest are white cards.

How many piles must have at least one white card?

A 4          B 3          C 2          D 1

**B is correct.**

First, work out how many white cards there are. There are 8 white cards as
15 cards – 2 red – 5 black = 8 white .

How many cards are in each pile? Each pile must have 3 cards in it, as 15 ÷ 5 = 3.

While it is possible that every pile has some white cards, the cards might be dealt in such a way that 2 piles have 3 white cards and 1 pile has 2 white cards. That would use all 8 white cards and leave 2 piles to be made up of the red and black cards. This means that only 3 piles **must** contain at least 1 white card.

**C and D are incorrect.** There cannot be white cards in only 1 or 2 piles as there are too many cards for 1 or 2 piles.

**A is incorrect.** There might be white cards in 4 piles but this is only possible.

### Practice questions

1 There are two brown lollies, four red lollies and seven green lollies in a black bag. Jasmin only likes to eat red lollies. How many lollies must she pull out of the bag so she is certain of getting a red lolly?

A 4

B 7

C 9

D 10

2 A cat rescue home has six large cages for the cats to sleep in at night. The owners of the cat home always share the cats as evenly as possible between the cages. If there are 15 cats at the home, how many cages have three cats in them?

A 1

B 2

C 3

D 4

## Calculations involving time

- Many questions will require you to work out how long someone is working and how many little jobs they can complete in that time. Knowing how to calculate the number of hours between times is important. So is knowing how many minutes are in an hour (60 minutes), half an hour (30 minutes) and a quarter of an hour (15 minutes).
- These questions will require good multiplication and division skills, so memorising your times tables is very important.
- Break these questions down. How long is the person working? How many things can be made per hour or per day? Use this information to find your answer.
- For example, if you know that a group can wash one car in 15 minutes, you can work out they can wash four cars in one hour. This helps if the rest of the question is measured in hours.

### SAMPLE QUESTION

Grandma Goodge can knit 25 rows of a scarf every hour that she knits. She likes to knit scarves with 150 rows in them. Grandma Goodge starts knitting a scarf at 9:00 am and stops for a half-hour lunch break at 12:00 noon. At what time will she finish knitting the scarf?

**A** 2:00 pm

**B** 2:30 pm

**C** 3:00 pm

**D** 3:30 pm

**D is correct.**

If Grandma Goodge can knit 25 rows in an hour, she can knit 50 rows in 2 hours, and so on until she knits 150 rows in 6 hours. We can find this using division also, as $150 \div 25 = 6$.

So it takes 6 hours to knit a scarf. If she starts at 9:00 am and goes without stopping she will finish 6 hours later at 3:00 pm. But she has a half-hour lunch break, so we need to add this time on.

She will finish at 3:30 pm.

### Practice questions

**1** Lee makes mugs out of clay to sell at her local market. She can make one mug every 10 minutes. On Thursday, Lee made mugs from 11:00 am to 3:00 pm, stopping for a half-hour lunch break at 1:00 pm. How many mugs did she make?

**A** 18

**B** 21

**C** 24

**D** 35

**2** Glenn plays cricket. He practises his bowling every day after school. He bowls three balls every minute but he takes a 10-minute break after every 10 minutes that he bowls. If he practises from 3:30 pm to 4:00 pm, how many balls does he bowl?

**A** 40

**B** 60

**C** 90

**D** 100

## Using a process of elimination

- Some questions will ask you to find the best option that will please every person in the question based on their likes and dislikes.
- Questions like this are best solved using a process of elimination. A list of all possible answers are crossed off as more information is learnt.

**SAMPLE QUESTION**

A group of gardeners were discussing which types of grass they liked to grow. The types of grass they discussed were buffalo, kikuyu, rye, zoysia and couch.

Amy likes buffalo, kikuyu and couch but not rye or zoysia. Billy likes rye, couch and kikuyu but no others. Cameron doesn't like couch but likes all the other types.

If they were to pick one grass that everyone liked, what would it be?

A  buffalo

B  kikuyu

C  zoysia

D  couch

**B is correct.**

Once you know what the question is asking for, you only need to write down the grasses once. Then you can cross off the grasses that aren't liked as you read through the information. After reading each bit of information, your list will have more lines through it.

Amy:       buffalo, kikuyu, ~~rye~~, ~~zoysia~~ and couch.

Billy:      ~~buffalo~~, kikuyu, ~~rye~~, ~~zoysia~~ and couch.

Cameron: ~~buffalo~~, kikuyu, ~~rye~~, ~~zoysia~~ and ~~couch~~.

Leaving you with kikuyu, the answer.

 **Practice questions**

**1** Four friends earnt some money washing a car. They were deciding which sports equipment they should buy with the money they earnt. They made the following statements.

**Gina:** 'I only want to play netball, basketball, tennis or soccer.'

**Andrew:** 'I want to play Aussie rules, basketball, tennis or soccer, but nothing else.'

**Kerry:** 'I don't like netball or tennis but I'll play anything else.'

**Mike:** 'I can't play soccer but I'll play everything else.'

Which equipment should they buy so that everyone is happy to play?

A  netball

B  basketball

C  soccer

D  Aussie rules

**2** Three friends were deciding which flavour cordial to buy.

Helena only likes lime, raspberry, mango, lemon and orange. Louisa only likes pineapple, orange, mango, raspberry, and cola. Belle likes everything except for raspberry and orange.

Which cordial should they buy?

A  raspberry

B  orange

C  lemon

D  mango

# Finding hidden information

- It can be hard to work out what has happened in questions where some people tell the truth and other people lie. But if we know some things about who is lying or telling the truth, we can use logical thinking skills to find out more.
- When told that one person is lying or one person is telling the truth, look for statements that contradict each other. If two people say opposing things then one of them must be lying and the other must be telling the truth.
- In the sample question below, only one person is lying. Gareth and Vinesh say opposing things, so one of them **must** be lying. This means the other two people must be telling the truth. Finding the statements that contradict each other is the quickest way to find the solutions in questions like this.

## SAMPLE QUESTION

Troy and his friends were playing by the pool when he noticed a pot plant had fallen in. Troy asked his friends who had knocked it into the pool.

Gareth said it was Vinesh. Vinesh said he didn't do it. Zara said it was Quinten and Quinten said Gareth was lying.

If only one person is lying, who knocked the pot plant into the pool?

A  Gareth

B  Vinesh

C  Zara

D  Quinten

**D is correct.**

Gareth and Vinesh say opposing things. So one of them must be the one that is lying. This means Zara must be telling the truth when she says that Quinten did it.

 **Practice questions**

① Mrs Kolinac had four children, Jannie, Tom, Chiara and Walt. When they were playing outside, a garden statue was knocked over and it broke. Mrs Kolinac asked each of the children what happened to the statue. They gave the following replies.

**Jannie:** 'Chiara broke it.'

**Tom:** 'Jannie broke it.'

**Chiara:** 'I didn't do it.'

**Walt:** 'Tom broke it.'

If Mrs Kolinac knows that only Chiara is telling the truth, who broke the statue?

A  Jannie

B  Tom

C  Chiara

D  Walt

② When playing football at school, a ball went over the fence and was lost in the bush. The teacher asked the students what happened to the ball.

Bernie said that Cinda lost it. Cinda said that Harald lost it. Harald said he didn't lose it and Marius said that Cinda was lying.

If only one of them is telling the truth, who lost the football?

A  Bernie

B  Cinda

C  Harald

D  Marius

## Solving 3D puzzles

- Solving three-dimensional (3D) puzzles on paper can be difficult. Learning how 3D objects can be rotated in your hands is important, so playing with blocks and Lego is very useful.
- When solving questions about 3D objects, try to turn pieces over in your head. It is best to turn pieces over in line with the sides of the piece. Pretend you have stuck a stick through the shape and turned it around that. What happens to each part of it? If there is a sloping part, where will that end up?
- Sometimes it is easier to turn one piece rather than another in your head, so try turning the object in the question if you can't turn the objects in the options.

### SAMPLE QUESTION

This solid is a piece of a 3D puzzle.

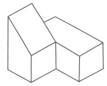

Which piece fits with it to make a cube?

A 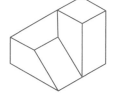   B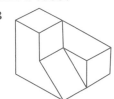

C 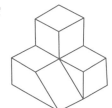   D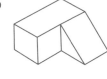

**B is correct.**

Turning the first piece over in your mind gives you a good idea as to how it might fit with the other pieces. Pretend you have stuck a stick through the side and turned it over. Focus on one section of the piece, maybe the sloped section or the gap in the front corner. Where will

this end up? Will this fit with any of the answers? The hidden edges that were on the top are shown with the dotted lines in the second diagram.

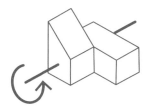   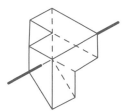

Here is the piece from B. The piece fits perfectly to make a cube.

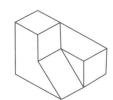   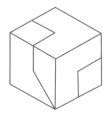

###  Practice questions

1 This solid is a piece of a 3D puzzle.

Which piece fits with it to make a cube?

A 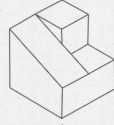   B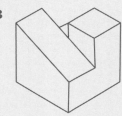

C    D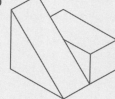

**2** This solid is a piece of a 3D puzzle.

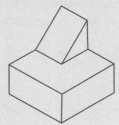

Which piece fits with it to make a cube?

A

B

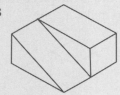

C

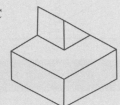

D

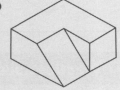

## Viewing objects from different sides

- There are many types of questions where you must be able to imagine the view of one or more objects from a particular side. Some questions show you a 3D view and some show you a 2D image.
- In each of the questions, there will be information in the question that can help you. For the sample question, place yourself on each side and think what you would see. Will you be able to see all the buildings? Which buildings will be in front of others? Which buildings are taller than the others?
- For the first practice question, does counting how many rows of windows there are help you work out how high the buildings are?
- For the second practice question, pick one shape and decide where the other shapes will be in relation to your shape.

### SAMPLE QUESTION

Four buildings are situated on a city block, surrounded by four streets.

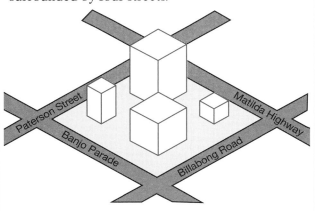

Which of the following is **not** a possible side view of the block from one of the streets?

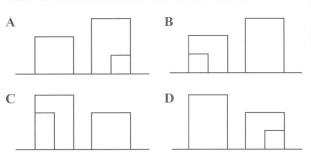

**D is correct.**

A is the view from Billabong Road. B is the view from Matilda Highway. C is the view from Banjo Parade. D is not the view from anywhere. If we look only at the larger buildings, we will notice that for them to be in the right place for D, we must be looking from Paterson Street or Banjo Parade. But from both of these streets, the small cube building would be hidden from view.

### Practice questions

**1** This is a view of four buildings from the front.

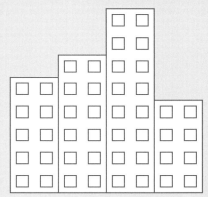

Which could be the view from the left-hand side?

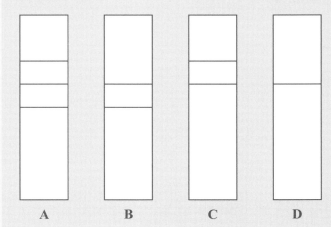

*Viewing objects from different sides*

**2** Four shapes have been drawn onto a box, as shown.

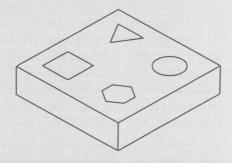

Which is the correct top view of the box?

A
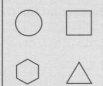

B

C
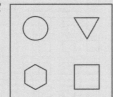

D
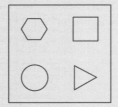

☞ **Answers and explanations on page 65**

## Reading timetables

- Many questions will require you to read a timetable. There are many types of timetable. Some will show hours of the day when people or things are or are not available.
- Always check what information is given and what information you can work out. For example, in the timetable in the sample question, every hour from 9 am to 6 pm is shown but only three are labelled: 9 am, 12 noon and 3 pm. You must label the other times yourself.
- Read the key to a timetable carefully.
- Often, you can answer questions like this using a process of elimination. For example, in the first practice question, look at the answer for A and check whether this works. If not, you can check with B, C and D.

### SAMPLE QUESTION

At the zoo, animal enclosures are open at different times of the day. The viewing times for the animals are shown below.

| Animal | 9 am | | | 12 noon | | | 3 pm | | |
|---|---|---|---|---|---|---|---|---|---|
| Elephants | | | | | | | | | |
| Lions | | | | | | | | | |
| Meercats | | | | | | | | | |
| Giraffes | | | | | | | | | |

☐ Open for viewing     ▨ Closed

Rita wanted to go to the zoo for 2 hours and see all the animals. Which time below is **not** a good time for her to go to the zoo?

A  10 am                B  11 am
C  2 pm                 D  3 pm

**D is correct.**

For Rita to see all the animals, each animal must be available (have a white box) in one of the two columns after the start time of Rita's trip.

If she goes at 10 am she will be able to see all the animals. We can see that in the two columns after 10 am, each animal is available for at least one hour.

| Animal | 9 am | 10 am | 11 am | 12 noon | 1 pm | 2 pm | 3 pm | 4 pm | 5 pm |
|---|---|---|---|---|---|---|---|---|---|
| Elephants | | | | | | | | | |
| Lions | | | | | | | | | |
| Meercats | | | | | | | | | |
| Giraffes | | | | | | | | | |

☐ Open for viewing     ▨ Closed

If she goes at 11 am she will see all the animals.

If she goes at 2 pm she will see all the animals.

If she goes at 3 pm she will not be able to see the elephants as the enclosure is not open between 3 pm and 5 pm.

She should not go at 3 pm.

### 🗘 Practice questions

1  The teachers Mr White, Mrs Black and Mr Brown want to have a meeting together. For this to happen, they must be on break at the same time. Here is the timetable for the teachers.

| Teacher | 8 am | | | | 12 noon | | | |
|---|---|---|---|---|---|---|---|---|
| Mr White | | | | | | | | |
| Miss Green | | | | | | | | |
| Mrs Black | | | | | | | | |
| Mr Pink | | | | | | | | |
| Mr Brown | | | | | | | | |

☐ Teaching     ▨ On break

When can the three teachers meet?
A  9 am to 10 am
B  11 am to 12 noon
C  12 noon to 1 pm
D  2 pm to 3 pm

## Reading timetables

**2** Zeno is going to a holiday camp to learn about science and maths. He is only going on Monday, Thursday and Friday. Each subject goes all day.

| Subject | Available |
| --- | --- |
| Infinity | Monday, Wednesday and Friday |
| The Planets | Tuesday, Thursday and Friday |
| The Sun | Wednesday and Thursday |
| Geometry | Tuesday, Wednesday and Friday |
| The Circle | Monday, Tuesday and Wednesday |
| Fractions | Tuesday and Thursday |

If he definitely wants to learn about Infinity and Geometry, which other subject is he unable to choose?

**A** The Planets

**B** The Sun

**C** Fractions

**D** The Circle

☞ **Answers and explanations on page 65**

## Questions about graphs

- Reading graphs is a very important skill. There are many types of graphs and they can be drawn in many different ways. This book will focus mainly on bar graphs and column graphs.
- Each bit of information given is usually important. In the sample question below, 24 people are represented by 12 little rectangles. This helps us work out how many people are represented by each rectangle.
- For a column graph, always read the labels on the axes and the key, which will tell you a bit about what the columns represent.

### SAMPLE QUESTION

A class of 24 students was shown paintings by four artists. Each student was asked to pick their favourite artist. They then created this graph to show the results.

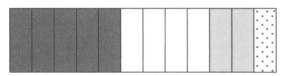

Matisse was the most popular artist and Gauguin was four times as popular as Cezanne.

How many people liked Picasso, the other artist?

**A** 1      **B** 2      **C** 4      **D** 5

**C is correct.**

We must find out two things to get to the answer here. Which rectangles represent each artist? How many people are represented by each rectangle?

The dark purple must represent Matisse as he is the most popular. Gauguin must have four times as many rectangles as Cezanne, so the white rectangles must represent Gauguin, and Cezanne must be the spots. Picasso must then be the light purple.

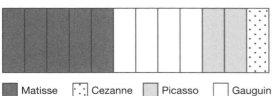

There are 12 rectangles to represent the 24 students of the class. This means that each rectangle stands for 2 students, as $2 \times 12 = 24$.

Picasso is represented by two rectangles. So four people picked Picasso as their favourite artist, as $2 \times 2$ rectangles = 4.

### Practice questions

1. Joseph counted the number of native trees in his school playground. He found four types of tree and made this graph.

There were more waratahs than any other tree. There were half as many banksia as there were wattle.

If there were 60 trees altogether, how many bottlebrush were there in the playground?

**A** 8      **B** 12      **C** 15      **D** 16

2. Jaime, Kira and Esther put their spelling marks for each test on a graph. However, they forgot to label the columns with their names.

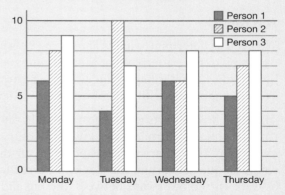

They remembered some things though:
- Kira and Esther scored the same on one of the daily tests.
- Kira was the only one to score 10 in a test.

What is the total of all Esther's marks?

**A** 21      **B** 31      **C** 22      **D** 32

# Identifying and following a pattern

- Patterns come in all different types and many questions can be asked about them. The questions in this book will focus mainly on rotating shapes and switching colours in those shapes.
- So, for each question, ask yourself what is happening to the shapes in each step of the pattern. Are the shapes rotating? Are the shapes moving in a line? What is happening to the colour in the shapes? Is it moving between them or staying in the same shapes?
- If you can answer these questions, you should be able to recognise a pattern and use that to help you answer the question.

## SAMPLE QUESTION

Each step in a pattern is made up of two shapes. The first three steps are shown below.

Which of the options below shows the next step in the pattern?

A     B

C     D

**A is correct.**

We need to determine what is happening between each step of the pattern. What is happening to the little arrow? What is happening to the big arrow? What is happening with the colour?

The little arrow starts pointing to the right and rotates a quarter turn in a clockwise direction every step. The big arrow starts pointing up, then rotates a quarter turn in the clockwise direction as well. The colour swaps between the big and small arrow each time.

So the next step should have a small purple arrow pointing up and a big white arrow pointing to the left. The answer is A.

## Practice questions

**1** Each step in a pattern is made up of two shapes. The first three steps are shown below.

Which of the options below shows the next step in the pattern?

A     B

C     D

**2** The first three steps are shown below.

  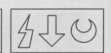

What is the next step in the pattern?

A     B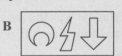

C     D

**1** Four buildings are on a street.

Which is the view of the four buildings from the right-hand side?

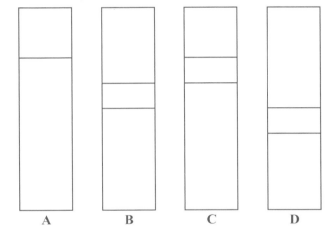

| A | B | C | D |

**2** Kangaroos are mainly left-handed. They use their right hand for strength but they use their left hand for tasks that need precision.

Which statement best expresses the main idea of the text?

A Kangaroos are mainly left-handed.

B Kangaroos use their left hand for precision tasks.

C Kangaroos are the largest marsupials on Earth.

D Kangaroos use their right hand for strength.

**3** When Gya was learning to play the clarinet, her music teacher told her: 'To have even a chance of passing the clarinet exam you must have practised for at least 50 hours.'

If Gya's music teacher is correct, which of these statements must be true?

A All the students who have practised for 50 hours will pass the clarinet exam.

B None of the students who have practised for less than 50 hours will pass the clarinet exam.

C Only the students who have practised for less than 50 hours will pass the clarinet exam.

D Some of the students who have practised for less than 50 hours will pass the clarinet exam.

**4** The following solid is one piece of a 3D puzzle.

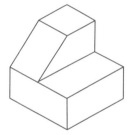

Which solid can be paired with it to make a cube?

A 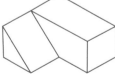    B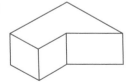

C     D

**5** Carter has made a sign and plans to stand holding it outside the local wetlands. The sign says: 'The expert report says the wetlands are in danger! We must save the wetlands!'

Which assumption did Carter make when he wrote the sign?

**A** We must save the wetlands.

**B** The wetlands are in danger.

**C** Saving the wetlands is a good thing.

**D** Saving the wetlands is not necessary.

**6** Three friends want to share a pizza. There are four possible toppings: Hawaiian, Cheese, Vegetarian and Supreme. Samantha likes everything except for Vegetarian. Lincoln likes everything except for Supreme. Glen only likes Hawaiian and Supreme.

Which pizza should the friends get so everyone is happy?

**A** Hawaiian

**B** Cheese

**C** Vegetarian

**D** Supreme

**7** A teacher found some money at a desk where four students sat. When she asked whose it was, this is what they said:

**David:** 'It's mine!'

**Tanya:** 'No, it's mine!'

**Mary:** 'Well, it's not David's or Tanya's.'

**Roger:** 'It's Mary's money.'

If two students are telling the truth and two are lying, whose money is it?

**A** David

**B** Tanya

**C** Mary

**D** Roger

**8** Mr Robinson tells the choir: 'There will be a special assembly on Friday to celebrate the school's anniversary but only those students who come to the lunchtime meeting today will be allowed to sing at the assembly.'

**Eli:** 'Oh no, Mum's picking me up at lunchtime today to go to the dentist! I won't be allowed to sing at the assembly.'

**Lily:** 'I'll be going to the lunchtime meeting so I'll definitely be singing at the assembly.'

If the information in the box is true, whose reasoning is correct?

**A** Eli only

**B** Lily only

**C** Both Eli and Lily

**D** Neither Eli nor Lily

**9** An officer from the water police said in a television interview: 'Lifejackets are the most important item of safety on a boat. Wearing a lifejacket can save your life. We recommend anyone boating in a recreational vessel should wear one at all times.'

Which one of these statements, if true, best supports the officer's claim?

**A** Vessels must carry enough life jackets for everyone.

**B** Seven out of ten people who drown while boating are not wearing a lifejacket.

**C** Lifejackets are also known as personal flotation devices.

**D** The water police have launched a campaign to encourage boaters to wear lifejackets.

**10** A group of people were asked to pick their favourite ice-cream flavour out of chocolate, mint, strawberry and vanilla.

Mint was the least liked flavour.

Twice as many people liked strawberry than liked vanilla.

More people liked chocolate than strawberry.

Which sector graph shows this information the best?

A

B

C

D
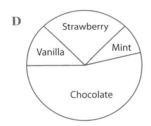

**11** Bella is in the local library. Her brother asked her to pick up a book for him about keeping goldfish. He told her he saw the one he wants in the local library. He said it has a blue cover.

**Bella:** 'This book about goldfish has a blue cover. It must be the one he wants!'

Which one of the following sentences shows the mistake Bella has made?

A There might be more than one book about goldfish with a blue cover.

B Even if the book is about goldfish, it might not have a blue cover.

C Bella's brother might now prefer a book about keeping cats.

D The book might be in the bookshop, not the library.

**12** No matter how old you are, it's important to take care of your teeth. Brushing your teeth twice a day helps keep them healthy. Visiting a dentist is important too. The dentist will check your teeth and clean them.

Which statement best expresses the main idea of the text?

A Visiting a dentist is important.

B You must take care of your teeth.

C An adult has 32 teeth.

D Brush your teeth twice a day.

**13** Chantelle has four chickens: Pamela, Dawn, Henrietta and Velma. She wants to give the two best layers to her sister's family. She counts the number of eggs each chicken lays over three weeks. The best layers are the ones that lay the most eggs in that time.

| Chicken | Week 1 | Week 2 | Week 3 |
|---------|--------|--------|--------|
| Pamela | 4 | 4 | 5 |
| Dawn | 3 | 6 | 5 |
| Henrietta | 4 | 5 | 5 |
| Velma | 6 | 2 | 3 |

Which chickens will Chantelle give to her sister?

A Pamela and Dawn

B Dawn and Henrietta

C Henrietta and Velma

D Pamela and Henrietta

**14** Archer is talking to his mum about what to get his brother for his birthday.

**Archer:** 'He'd really like that new computer game.'

**Archer's mum:** 'Okay. And if we can't find the computer game, then we can get him a laser-tag voucher. But if we do get the computer game, then we'll also get him a book instead of that electronic piggy bank.'

If they do not give Archer's brother a laser-tag voucher for his birthday, what do they give him?

A a computer game and a book

B an electronic piggy bank only

C a book and an electronic piggy bank

D a computer game only

**15** The pattern on the left is made of 16 square tiles, all the same. Then three tiles broke and needed to be replaced. The three spaces are shown in the picture on the right.

Which way of placing the tile is **not** used?

    A          B          C          D

15 MIN

**1** Four students competed in a school science competition. Jamie scored more than Clair, Moira scored less than Rodney and Clair scored more than Rodney.

What position did Moira finish?

A 1st

B 2nd

C 3rd

D 4th

**2** Jackson and Sofia are comparing their lunches.

**Jackson:** 'I've got a vegemite sandwich again. That's three days in a row now.'

**Sofia:** 'You must really like vegemite!'

**Jackson:** 'No, not really. Dad just hasn't had a chance to get to the grocery store.'

Which assumption has Sofia made to draw her conclusion?

A Jackson really likes vegemite.

B Jackson's dad hasn't done the grocery shopping.

C Jackson has had a vegemite sandwich for lunch for three days in a row.

D Jackson would only have vegemite so often if he really liked vegemite.

**3** Thomas goes away with two blue shirts, three green shirts and four yellow shirts. All the shirts are at the bottom of his bag. Thomas wants to pick out a green shirt to wear for the day.

How many shirts must Thomas pick so that he is certain to get a green one?

A 3 　　　 B 5 　　　 C 7 　　　 D 9

**4** A leopard is large with thick legs and brown spots. A cheetah is thinner than a leopard with long legs and black spots.

**Willow:** 'Oh look! That must be a leopard. It has spots.'

**Jun:** 'No, it can't be! It's not very large.'

If the information in the box is true, whose reasoning is correct?

A Willow only

B Jun only

C Both Willow and Jun

D Neither Willow nor Jun

**5** Four people are working today at Brown Books. The table shows when they are working.

| | 8 am | | | | 12 noon | | | 4 pm | | | | 8 pm | | |
|---|---|---|---|---|---|---|---|---|---|---|---|---|---|---|
| Leon | | | | | | | | | | | | | | |
| Nino | | | | | | | | | | | | | | |
| Bill | | | | | | | | | | | | | | |
| Pavel | | | | | | | | | | | | | | |

 Not working 　　　 Working

The boss puts more people on during the busy periods in the shop. Who is **not** working today during the busy period?

A Leon

B Nino

C Bill

D Pavel

**6** Four shapes are drawn on the top of a square box shown below.

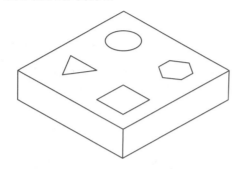

Which picture shows the correct top view of the box?

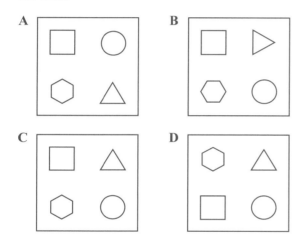

A

B

C

D

**7** A wildlife volunteer said in a radio interview: 'Temporary fencing must be installed to protect a kookaburra hollow in the Bird Bay Reserve. It will soon be breeding season and the two mating birds there have previously lost some of their eggs to predators.'

Which one of these statements, if true, best supports the volunteer's claim?

**A** Kookaburras are native to Australia and New Guinea.

**B** A recent survey has revealed that kookaburra numbers are in decline.

**C** Rat poison and slug bait can stay in the food chain and kill native wildlife.

**D** There are already nesting boxes in the reserve for parrots and possums.

**8** Look at the four-piece puzzle below.

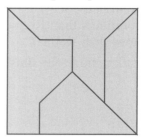

Which of the pieces below is **not** one of the four pieces? The pieces may be rotated only. They **cannot** be reflected.

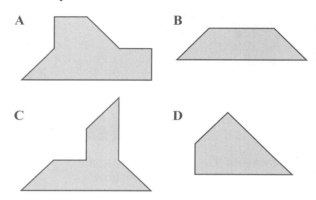

A

B

C

D

**9** Rocky Range Regional Botanic Garden is open again for visitors after the damage caused by the windstorm before Christmas. Garden visiting hours are daily from 8 am to 5 pm. Plus the volunteer nursery is also open on Saturdays from 2 to 4 pm and Tuesdays from 9 am to 12 noon. So come in and buy a plant!

If all of the above information is true, which one of the sentences below **cannot** be true?

**A** Kala arrived at the Garden at 10 am on Monday and stayed for 3 hours but she did not buy a plant.

**B** Kala visited the Garden between 2 and 4 pm on Tuesday and bought a plant.

**C** Kala arrived at the Garden at 10 am on Tuesday but she did not buy a plant.

**D** Kala visited the Garden on Saturday and didn't leave until 3 pm after she bought a plant.

☞ **Answers and explanations on pages 68–70**

**10** A shoemaker starts work at 9:00 am and finishes at 5:00 pm every day. He takes a half-hour lunch break at 1:00 pm. If it takes him 15 minutes to make one shoe, how many complete pairs of shoes can he make in one work day?

A 15     B 16     C 30     D 32

**11** Even though platypuses are mammals, they lay eggs. This makes them monotremes. Platypuses are one of only five monotreme species still surviving in the world.

Which statement best expresses the main idea of the text?

A Platypuses lay eggs.

B Echidnas lay eggs.

C Platypuses are monotremes.

D There are four species of echidnas.

**12** Each step in a pattern is made up of two shapes. The first three steps in the pattern are shown below.

What is the next step in the pattern?

A      B

C      D

**13** Mum, Grandpa and Aria are planning what to plant next in their garden. Mum says she wants to plant basil, roses, lavender, parsley and rosemary. Grandpa says he wants to plant passionfruit, rosemary and thyme. Aria wants to plant basil, tomatoes, parsley, thyme and carrots.

What does Mum want to plant that neither Grandpa nor Aria wants to plant?

A basil and roses

B roses and lavender

C passionfruit and thyme

D lavender and parsley

**14** A camp offers craft courses. Edren must pick one course only from each list.

| List 1 | List 2 | List 3 |
|---|---|---|
| Scrapbooking | Knitting | Woodwork |
| Sewing | Clothes dyeing | Sewing |
| Painting | Drawing | Modelling |
| Drawing | Woodwork | Cross-stitch |
| Knitting | Cross-stitch | Painting |

Edren wants to choose Modelling and Woodwork.

Which course can she **not** choose?

A Knitting

B Cross-stitch

C Scrapbooking

D Painting

**15** George and Talia are best friends. They have just arrived at the Reptile Park and are deciding what to do.

**George:** 'The map says between 2 and 3 pm you can get a photo holding a snake. Eeek! How scary!'

**Talia:** 'Okay, we won't do that then.'

**George:** 'No, let's do it!'

Which assumption has Talia made to draw her conclusion?

A George does not want to be scared.

B George wants to hold a snake.

C They won't hold a snake for a photo.

D George says it's scary to hold a snake.

**1** The following is the front view of four buildings on a street.

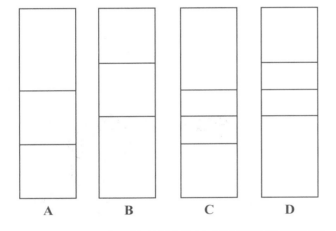

Which of the following could be the view of the four buildings from the left side?

A    B    C    D

**2** While three brothers were meant to be asleep, one of them sneaked out to the fridge and ate a big slice of chocolate cake. In the morning they were questioned by their mum.

Chico said Harpo stole the cake. Harpo said Groucho stole the cake and Groucho said he didn't steal the cake at all.

Only one of the brothers is a liar. Who stole the cake?

A  Chico
B  Harpo
C  Groucho
D  There is not enough information to decide.

**3** The dog trainer said: 'To have any chance of moving up to the next grade, your dog must be able to sit on command, wait on the spot while you walk away and then come to you when you call.'

**Livvy:** 'Pudge can do all of those things easily so we are sure to move up to the next grade!'

Which one of the following sentences shows the mistake Livvy has made?

A  Working with your dog is a lot of fun.
B  There are a lot of dogs in the training class.
C  Doing the minimum does not guarantee moving to the next grade.
D  Some owners do not practise with their dogs between training classes.

**4** Remy says: 'My father thinks it is rude to use a mobile phone when you are with other people. He says the people in front of you are more important—but by looking at your mobile phone, you make them feel less important.'

Which one of these statements, if true, best supports Remy's father's claim?

A  Mobile devices are loaded with useful information if you need to check something during a conversation.
B  Many teens are addicted to their mobile phones and feel they cannot survive without them.
C  Mobile devices help people stay better connected.
D  A study found that the presence of a mobile phone during a conversation made people feel less connected.

**5** The following solid is one piece of a 3D puzzle.

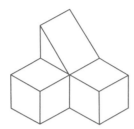

Which solid can be paired with it to make a cube?

A 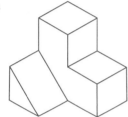 B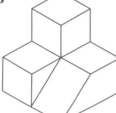

C 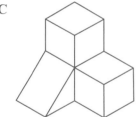 D

**6** A developer wants to build a fun park surrounding Crab Island. He says a fun park would support the local community by bringing tourists to the island.

Which one of these statements, if true, would **weaken** the developer's claim?

A A fun park would contribute to the Crab Island local economy.

B A fun park would destroy the marine life that is important to the culture and way of life of the local community.

C Crab Island is a natural wonder and home to unique and rare sea birds, land crabs and marine life.

D Crab Island is one of the few unspoilt tropical environments left in the world.

**7** Three friends are deciding what sport to watch on TV. Swimming, golf, rugby league, netball and soccer are all on, but the friends can only watch one of them.

Timo likes all sports except for golf. Brenton will watch all sports except for netball and swimming. Patty watches swimming, golf, rugby league and netball, but doesn't like anything else.

What sport should the friends watch so everyone gets to watch something they like?

A swimming
B rugby league
C netball
D soccer

**8** Elephants can lift something one and a half times as heavy as they are. So one elephant could lift an elephant and a half. But ants can lift something 50 times heavier than they are. So one ant could lift 50 ants. That means the ant is stronger than the elephant!

Which statement best expresses the main idea of the text?

A Elephants are strong.
B One ant can lift 50 ants.
C An elephant is the largest land mammal.
D An ant is stronger than an elephant.

**9** When Matilda entered an obstacle race the organiser told her: 'To have even a chance of getting a prize you must clear at least ten obstacles along the course.'

If the organiser is correct, which one of these statements will be true?

A All the entrants who clear ten obstacles will win a prize.

B Only the entrants who clear less than ten obstacles will win a prize.

C None of the entrants who clear less than ten obstacles will win a prize.

D Some of the entrants who clear less than ten obstacles will win a prize.

**10** The bar graph below was used to represent the results of a survey on people's favourite big cat.

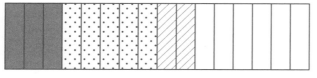

Tiger   Lion   Panther   Cougar

If 6 more people liked lions than panthers, how many people were surveyed altogether?

A 16
B 32
C 48
D 64

**11** Summer is at the park with her brother, Ari.

**Summer:** 'Mum said she will be angry if we don't get home by five o'clock.'

**Ari:** 'It's nearly five now. We'd better hurry home.'

Which assumption has Ari made to draw his conclusion?

A They should hurry home now.
B They should not make their mother angry.
C Their mum will be angry if they are not home by five o'clock.
D It doesn't matter if their mum gets angry.

**12** Whenever his favourite team wins, it always puts Poppy's neighbour in a good mood. And when Poppy's neighbour is in a good mood, he always plays his music really loudly.

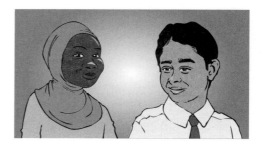

**Poppy:** 'If my neighbour's team wins next Saturday, he's sure to play his music really loudly!'

**Kamal:** 'Your neighbour is playing his music really loudly now. His team must have won today!'

If the information in the box is true, whose reasoning is correct?

A Poppy only
B Kamal only
C Both Poppy and Kamal
D Neither Poppy nor Kamal

**13** The pattern on the left is made of 16 square tiles, all the same. Then three tiles broke and needed to be replaced. The three spaces are shown in the picture on the right.

 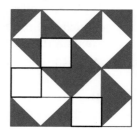

Which way of placing the tile is **not** used?

A       B       C       D

**14** A scientist said in a newspaper interview: 'Tree plantations are not a solution for climate change. In fact, large-scale tree plantations with only one species of tree may be doing more harm than good to the climate. That's because these single-species plantations do not store carbon in the same way that mixed old-growth forests do.'

Which one of these statements, if true, best supports the scientist's claim?

**A** A mix of plant species grows better together than a group of a single species.

**B** Old-growth, diverse forests store carbon for centuries.

**C** Studies have shown that single-species plantations emit more carbon than they absorb.

**D** Forests are like complex machines with millions of connected parts all working together.

**15** Twenty chocolate eggs are hidden in Cosmo's backyard for his friends and him to find. When they are found, 20 eggs are hidden in the front yard too. The person who finds the most eggs wins a prize.

Here is a table showing how many eggs each person found. It is missing two bits of information.

| Name | Eggs found in back yard | Eggs found in front yard |
|---|---|---|
| Cosmo | 4 | 1 |
| Dante | 2 | |
| Melissa | 1 | 5 |
| Parvati | 7 | |
| Joseph | 6 | 2 |

Dante wins the prize for finding the most eggs. He beat Parvati by one egg.

How many eggs did Dante find in the front yard?

**A** 9

**B** 10

**C** 11

**D** 12

Answers and explanations on pages 70–72

**1** Three friends are sitting at the table shown.

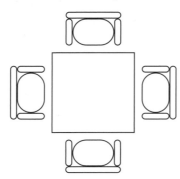

Ryan is sitting next to Marissa and Marissa is sitting next to Summer.

What must be true?

**A** Ryan is sitting opposite the empty chair.

**B** Marissa is sitting opposite the empty chair.

**C** Ryan and Summer are sitting next to each other.

**D** Ryan is sitting on Marissa's right.

**2** Bodhi wants a computer game. He sees it for sale online for the special price of $39.95 for an instant download. He goes to his favourite game store at the shopping mall to compare the price. He finds that the price is the same but the game store will give him reward points to put towards his next purchase. They are currently out of stock but he can pay for the game and wait two weeks for new stock to arrive. He checks one more general store. They have it in stock for $49.95 and it comes with a free book.

If the above information is correct, which one of the following is **not** possible?

**A** Bodhi pays $39.95 for an instant download of the game and gets reward points.

**B** Bodhi pays $39.95 for the game, gets reward points and waits for two weeks to collect the game.

**C** Bodhi pays the higher price to take the game home today and gets a free book.

**D** Bodhi pays $39.95 for the game and gets an instant download.

**3** A bag contains 3 green lollies, 5 white lollies and 6 red lollies. Colin cannot see inside the bag but knows that he wants to eat a white lolly.

What is the smallest number of lollies that Colin must take from the bag to make sure that he gets a white lolly?

**A** 4     **B** 6     **C** 9     **D** 10

**4** Strap on a helmet whenever you ride a bike. Your head can be badly injured in a bike accident but a good helmet will protect your head from injury.

Which statement best expresses the main idea of the text?

**A** Your head can be injured.

**B** Don't ride too close to others.

**C** Wear a helmet when you ride a bike.

**D** A helmet protects your head.

**5** A local art centre offers the classes in the timetable below. Classes all run at the same time, so you cannot do two classes on the same day.

| Class | Days on offer |
|---|---|
| Pottery | Monday, Friday |
| Sculpture | Tuesday, Wednesday, Thursday |
| Drawing | Monday, Thursday, Friday |
| Painting | Tuesday, Wednesday, Friday |

Peta wants to go to classes on Tuesday and Friday.

Which pair of classes is Peta **not** able to go to?

**A** Pottery and Sculpture

**B** Sculpture and Painting

**C** Pottery and Drawing

**D** Sculpture and Drawing

**6** Four shapes are drawn on the top of a square box shown below.

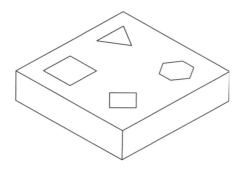

Which picture shows the correct top view of the box?

A

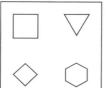

B

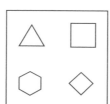

C

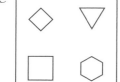

D

**7** Zoe, Mimi, Isaac and David are all in a debating club. The club captain has just told them: 'If Zoe can't make it to Friday's debate, then Mimi will take her place on the team. But if Zoe can make it, then Isaac will be on the team instead of David.'

If Mimi does not debate on Friday, which of the other three will be in the team?

A Isaac and David

B Zoe only

C David only

D Zoe and Isaac

**8** Look at the following four-piece puzzle.

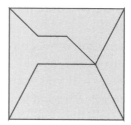

You have this piece.

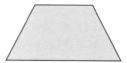

Which other pieces do you need to complete the puzzle? You may rotate pieces but you **cannot** flip/reflect them.

A

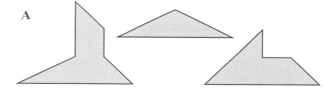

B

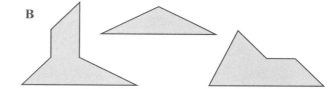

C

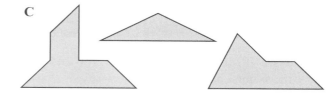

D

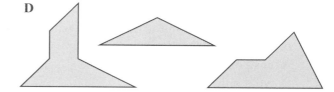

**9** The pet store had a sign in the window:

'Adorable kittens instore now! Get in quick if you want one!'

Which assumption is needed for the sign's conclusion to work?

A  Get in quickly if you want to buy a kitten.

B  The kittens are adorable and instore now.

C  The kittens will sell out quickly.

D  The pet store wants to sell all the kittens.

**10** Colleen washes dogs each Saturday to get some pocket money. She charges $10 per dog. Colleen washes 3 dogs every hour. If Colleen washes dogs non-stop from 8:00 am to 10:40 am, how much money does she make?

A  $60

B  $70

C  $80

D  $90

**11**

Whenever Josh and Mila's mum buys a new dress, it's always because there is a sale on.

**Josh:** 'If Mum buys a new dress, you know there must be a sale on.'

**Mila:** 'But if she doesn't buy a new dress, it doesn't mean there isn't a sale on.'

If the information in the box is true, whose reasoning is correct?

A  Josh only

B  Mila only

C  Both Josh and Mila

D  Neither Josh nor Mila

**12** The first three steps of a pattern are shown below.

What is the next step in the pattern?

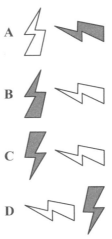

A

B

C

D

**13** An advertisement in the newspaper said:

Maintain your smoke alarm.

Ensure it works when you need it most!

Up In Smoke—the name you can trust in smoke alarms.

Which one of these statements, if true, best supports the advertisement's claim?

A  There are different types of smoke alarms for people who are deaf or hard of hearing.

B  Old smoke alarms should be dropped off at Community Recycling Centres so they are disposed of safely and in an environmentally friendly way.

C  Up in Smoke is a company that manufactures and sells smoke alarms.

D  The Fire and Rescue Department recommends smoke alarms should be vacuum cleaned every six months.

  ☞ **Answers and explanations on pages 72–74**

**14** Taki and Lucy use a cipher to hide messages that they send to each other. The cipher swaps the first and second letters around, then the third and fourth, and so on, with each pair of letters in the message. If there is an odd number of letters the last letter stays in its place.

For example:     HELLO MY FRIEND
Is written as:     EHLLM OF YIRNED

Taki wants to send the message SEE YOU AT SCHOOL to Lucy. What should he write?

**A** LOOHCS TA OUY EES
**B** ESE OYU TA CSOHLO
**C** ESE YUO AT CSHOLO
**D** ESY EUO TA CSOHLO

**15**

**Oscar:** 'I know that eleven teachers at my school drive to school but I only saw eight cars in the staff car park this morning. So some of the teachers must have walked today.'

Which one of the following sentences shows the mistake Oscar has made?

**A** He did not say which teachers must have walked to school.
**B** Some of the teachers might be trying to get fit.
**C** He did not say which teachers normally drive to school.
**D** Some of the teachers might not have driven or walked to school.

**1** Five balls were placed in a straight line as shown.

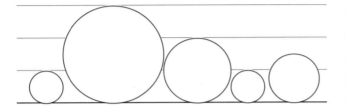

Which of the following is the view of the balls from the right-hand side?

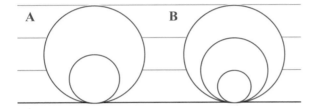

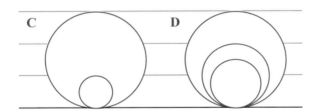

**2** Ollie's 5-year-old brother has a star chart for good behaviour. When there are ten stars he can choose a special treat. Ollie's mother gives him a star when he gets all his spelling correct in a test.

**Jenna:** 'Ollie says his brother got a treat last Friday. His little brother must have got all his spelling words correct.'

**Michaela:** 'If Ollie's mother lets Ollie's brother choose a treat this Friday, he must have earned ten stars.'

If the information in the box is true, whose reasoning is correct?

**A** Jenna only

**B** Michaela only

**C** Both Jenna and Michaela

**D** Neither Jenna nor Michaela

**3** Johanna, Taylah and Billy collect postcards. Billy has collected postcards from around Australia, New Zealand, the United Kingdom, Japan and Denmark. Johanna has postcards from Australia, New Zealand, Indonesia, Germany, Switzerland, Spain and Italy. Taylah has postcards from the USA, Vietnam, Thailand, Australia, Germany, Switzerland, France, Greece and Italy. She even has one card from South Africa.

Which countries does Johanna have postcards from that neither Billy nor Taylah has?

**A** South Africa and Greece

**B** Germany and Switzerland

**C** Spain and Indonesia

**D** Italy and Greece

**4** The following solid is one piece of a 3D puzzle.

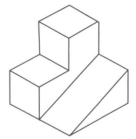

Which solid goes with it to make a cube?

**A**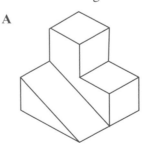

**B**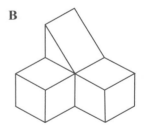

**C**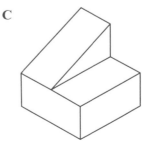

**D**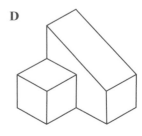

☞ **Answers and explanations on pages 74–75**

**5** The netball coach told Harriet that to have any chance of improving her goal shooting skills she must practise for at least three sessions a week for an hour each time. Harriet currently practises every Tuesday for 90 minutes.

Which conclusion **cannot** be true?

A Harriet continues practising on Tuesday for 90 minutes and does not improve her goal shooting.

B Harriet continues practising on Tuesdays but increases to two hours and improves her playing.

C Harriet decides to only practise for one hour on a Wednesday and does not improve her playing.

D Harriet devotes a lot more time to netball practice and improves her goal shooting.

**6** Four friends are going on an adventure holiday together. There are five types of holiday they can choose from: surfing, waterskiing, snowboarding, rock climbing or bushwalking.

Cormoran likes all activities except for rock climbing. Robyn loves to go surfing, snowboarding and bushwalking but doesn't like anything else. Midge doesn't enjoy bushwalking and Charlotte doesn't like surfing at all.

Which type of holiday should they book so that everyone is happy?

A surfing

B waterskiing

C snowboarding

D bushwalking

**7** A farmer went to feed his herd of cattle but found that they had all escaped through an open gate. He asked his four workers who left the gate open. They gave the following replies.

**Kevin:** 'Declan left it open.'

**Declan:** 'Maurice left it open.'

**Maurice:** 'Declan is lying. I didn't leave it open.'

**Bella:** 'All I know is Kevin didn't do it.'

If only one of the workers is telling the truth, who left the gate open?

A Kevin      B Declan

C Maurice      D Bella

**8** Urgent action is needed to save the Southern Corroboree frog from extinction. The Southern Corroboree frog is a critically endangered species of frog only found in Mount Kosciuszko National Park in NSW. Frogs and tadpoles are a vital part of the food chain, eating insects and being food for other animals. Taronga Zoo, among other organisations, has been involved in a captive breeding program, breeding and releasing the frogs into fungus-free areas of the national park in the hope the frogs can survive.

Which statement best expresses the main idea of the text?

A Southern Corroboree frogs are dying due to a fungus that also kills other amphibians.

B Urgent action is needed to save the Southern Corroboree frog from extinction.

C Captive breeding programs are helping by releasing frogs into the wild.

D The Southern Corroboree frog is a critically endangered species.

**9** Mud bricks have been used to build homes for thousands of years. Mud bricks are made by mixing earth, water and straw. The mix is dried out in moulds in the sun. Mud bricks are better than concrete bricks in many ways. They are cheaper to make. They keep temperatures inside the home cooler. They are environmentally friendly.

Which statement **weakens** the above claim?

A Mud-brick homes are fire safe.

B The mud brick is the oldest building material in the world.

C Mud-brick homes must be built on waterproof foundations.

D Owner builders can make their own mud bricks or buy commercially made ones.

**10** Blinx, Qizz, Woop and Zing are four shops. The sales made by the four shops for 2 years are shown in the table. Each company name has been replaced by a number.

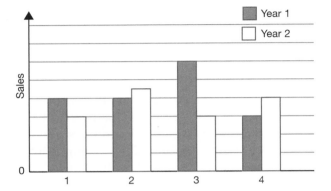

Use the information to answer the question.

■ Qizz increased their sales the most between the first and second years.

■ Woop made the most combined sales over both years.

■ Zing made the exact same combined sales as another company over the two years.

What is the correct order of the companies?

A Zing, Blinx, Woop, Qizz

B Qizz, Blinx, Woop, Zing

C Zing, Woop, Blinx, Qizz

D Zing, Qizz, Woop, Blinx

**11** Kangaroos are bigger than wallabies. Kangaroos can grow up to two metres tall while wallabies rarely grow taller than one metre. Kangaroos have longer legs than wallabies because they need to be faster to cover greater distances of open area. Wallabies live in forests or rocky areas.

**Suzuka:** 'That marsupial has short legs so it must be a wallaby.'

**Madison:** 'It's over a metre tall so it must be a kangaroo.'

If the information in the box is true, whose reasoning is correct?

A Suzuka only

B Madison only

C Neither Suzuka nor Madison

D Both Suzuka and Madison

**12** Toby and Scarlet are outside the school assembly hall.

**Toby:** 'Sana asked me to collect her school shoes. She left them lined up here with everyone else's shoes when she went inside the hall for dance. She says they are just normal black lace-ups.'

**Scarlet:** 'Sana's shoes will be the same size as mine as we are the same age and height. Here's a pair in my size. These must be Sana's!'

Which one of the following sentences shows the mistake Scarlet has made?

A Scarlet thinks Sana's shoes are normal black lace-ups but they might not be.

B Scarlet cannot assume she'll have the same-sized feet as Sana just because she's the same age and height.

C Someone else might have already collected Sana's shoes.

D Toby might not want to collect Sana's shoes.

☞ **Answers and explanations on pages 74–75**

**13** The Best Sprinter award goes to the athlete whose combined best time for the 100 m and 200 m is the smallest. The best times for each are shown below.

| Name | Best 100-m time | Best 200-m time |
|------|-----------------|-----------------|
| Matt | 11.0 | 20.0 |
| Rohan | 10.1 | 20.2 |
| Jesse | 10.5 | 19.9 |
| Carl | 9.9 | 21.0 |

Who won the best sprinter award?

**A** Matt

**B** Rohan

**C** Jesse

**D** Carl

**14** Dante, Meghan, Yuta and William play volleyball in the same mixed team. The coach has just announced that if Dante does not play in the next game, then Yuta will play. If Dante does play, then Meghan will play and not William.

So if Yuta does not play in the next game, which of the other three will play?

**A** Dante and Meghan

**B** Dante only

**C** Meghan and Yuta

**D** William and Meghan

**15** The pattern on the left is made of 16 square tiles, all the same. Three tiles broke and needed to be replaced. The three spaces are shown in the picture on the right.

 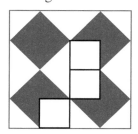

Which way of placing the tile is **not** used?

   A         B         C         D

**1** Daniel, Nico, Fernando and Sergio were in a car race. Fernando finished before Daniel, Nico finished before Fernando and Sergio finished after Fernando.

Who came second in the race?
**A** Daniel
**B** Nico
**C** Fernando
**D** Sergio

**2** Broccoli is rich in vitamins and minerals but when broccoli is chewed it gives off an aroma that some people don't like. To some people broccoli tastes bitter. Children are more sensitive to the smell and taste of broccoli than adults and their reaction is genetic, which means people can't help their disgust at the smell or taste of broccoli. So the next time an adult insists you eat your broccoli just say 'My genes are telling me not to eat it!'

Which of the following **weakens** the above claim?
**A** You really should try to eat broccoli even if it tastes terrible to you.
**B** You might not like the taste but the health benefits of eating broccoli are worth it.
**C** Broccoli is considered a superfood because it's so good for you.
**D** You can use cheese or soy sauce to mask the flavour of broccoli.

**3** Elizabeth has 14 red cards and 6 black cards. After shuffling the cards so they are in a random order, Elizabeth deals all of the cards out to four friends. She doesn't receive any cards herself.

How many of the friends must receive at least 1 red card?
**A** 1
**B** 2
**C** 3
**D** 4

**4** Daivik regularly uses garlic, mint, parsley, oregano, basil, thyme and rosemary in his cooking. Samir often uses coriander, dill, parsley, mint, tarragon and fennel. Amelia loves using thyme, rosemary, coriander, parsley, mint, fennel and garlic.

Which herbs does Samir like to use more often than Daivik and Amelia?
**A** coriander and rosemary
**B** fennel and dill
**C** fennel and parsley
**D** tarragon and dill

**5** Four shapes are drawn on the top of a square box shown below.

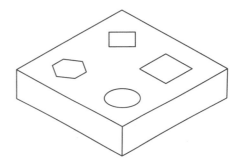

Which picture shows the correct top view of the box?

A     B

C 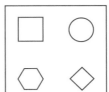    D

**6** The opening hours for four shops on a street are shown below.

| | 8 am | | | | 12 noon | | | | 4 pm | | | | |
|---|---|---|---|---|---|---|---|---|---|---|---|---|---|
| Rugs Galore | ▨ | ▨ | | | | | | | | | ▨ | ▨ | |
| Terry's Sports | | | | | ▨ | | | | | | | | |
| Computers Co | ▨ | | | | | | | ▨ | ▨ | | | | |
| Tables 'r' Us | | | | | | | | | | | ▨ | | |

☐ Open   ▨ Closed

Melanie wants to do her shopping in 2 hours. She needs to visit all the shops.

What time should she go shopping?

**A** 10 am – 12 noon

**B** 12 noon – 2 pm

**C** 2 pm – 4 pm

**D** 4 pm – 6 pm

**7** Sidney Nolan is a famous Australian artist. His artworks include an amazing series of paintings about the life of Ned Kelly painted between 1946 and 1947. These paintings show Nolan's sense of humour and the themes of injustice, family and betrayal set in the Australian bush.

If you have an opportunity to see the series in a gallery, make sure you give yourself plenty of time to examine each work. They are worth it.

Which of these statements, if true, most **strengthens** the above argument?

**A** Sidney Nolan is famous around the world.

**B** The series belongs to the National Gallery of Australia but tours nationally and internationally.

**C** The story of Ned Kelly makes an interesting topic for a series of artworks.

**D** Ned Kelly died in jail when he was executed for his crimes.

**8** Look at the following four-piece puzzle.

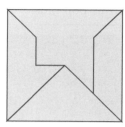

You have this piece.

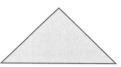

Which other pieces do you need to complete the puzzle? You may rotate pieces but you **cannot** flip/reflect them.

A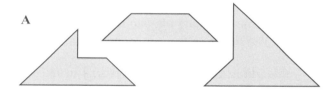

B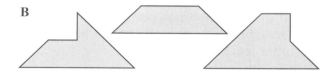

C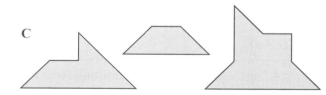

D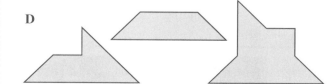

9 | A pop star is a famous singer or musician who performs pop music.

**Stevie:** 'To become a pop star you have to be a great dancer as well as a great singer.'

Which one of the following sentences shows the mistake Stevie has made?

A There are plenty of great pop stars who don't dance.

B Not every popular song has a dance video.

C Some pop stars play an instrument.

D The best pop songs become big hits.

10 Glenda is a bricklayer who works from 7:00 am to 3:00 pm every day. She has a half-hour lunch break, which starts at 12:00 noon. If she lays 120 bricks per hour, how many more bricks does she lay before lunch than after lunch?

A 230

B 250

C 300

D 360

11 | Ashley and Novak are babysitting Novak's little sister Mia, who is nine months old. Mia is asleep in her room. Novak and Ashley are standing outside the door to the room.

**Ashley:** 'I can hear her crying. We should go in and check on her.'

**Novak:** 'I can't hear her crying. Mum said to only go in if she's crying. She regularly wakes up and cries out during nap time but she goes back to sleep if you leave her alone. We need to wait. She might have gone back to sleep.'

If the information in the box is true, whose reasoning is correct?

A Ashley only

B Novak only

C Both Ashley and Novak

D Neither Ashley nor Novak

12 The first four steps in a pattern are shown.

1    2

3    4

What is the next step in the pattern?

A    B

C    D

13 **Isobel:** 'We're selling our old cubby house. My sister and I don't use it any more so we've listed it online. It's a raised cubby with a door and windows. We had a lot of fun in it when we were younger. Mum has taken it apart. It took her two hours!'

Which claim **weakens** Isobel's ability to sell her old cubby house?

A good condition

B staircase and ladder included

C recommended for children aged 1+

D minimum two hours of assembly required

**14** Mr Wilson asked his students their favourite colour. All his students picked either red, pink, yellow, green or blue.

More than half the students picked blue or red. More than a quarter of the students picked red or yellow. And more than a quarter of the students picked yellow or green.

Which sector graph is correct?

A
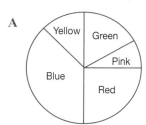

B
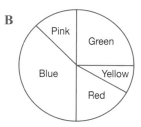

C
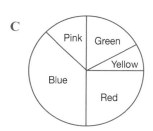

D
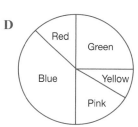

**15** Kanami's mother has said to choose two friends for tenpin bowling on ANZAC Day. Kanami has four close friends. They are Gretchen, Dom, Marcus and Will. Gretchen might not be able to go bowling as her family usually attends ANZAC Day services together. If Gretchen is not allowed to go bowling, then Kanami will invite Dom and not Marcus. If Gretchen does attend, then Marcus will be invited and not Will.

So if Gretchen is not allowed to go tenpin bowling, which of the other friends will be invited?

A Gretchen only

B Will and Dom

C Marcus and Will

D Dom and Marcus

**1** Six balls were placed in a straight line as shown.

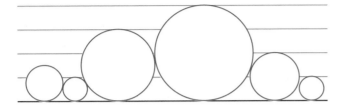

Which of the following is the view of the balls from the left-hand side?

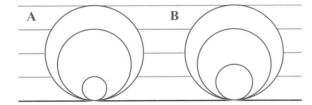

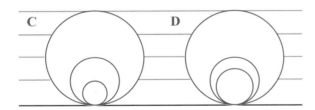

**2** The bowling alley opens from Tuesday to Sunday from 10 am to 6 pm. Chiho and Floyd visited during the school holidays.

Which of the sentences below **cannot** be true?

A  Chiho and Floyd went bowling at 11 am on Wednesday.

B  Chiho and Floyd went bowling between 4 pm and 5.30 pm on Thursday.

C  Chiho and Floyd went bowling at 11 am on Monday.

D  Chiho and Floyd went bowling until 6 pm on Sunday.

**3** **Aunty Denise:** 'To have any chance of getting the pavlova finished on Saturday before the guests arrive at 12 pm, I have to start baking by 9 am at the latest.'

**Uncle Jim:** 'We'll set the alarm for 9 am and you'll definitely have it made by 12.'

Which one of the following sentences shows the mistake Uncle Jim has made?

A  Aunty Denise needs at least three hours to get the pavlova finished.

B  A pavlova takes three hours to make.

C  He shouldn't rely on an alarm going off on time.

D  He doesn't understand how tricky it is to make pavlova.

**4** The following solid is one piece of a 3D puzzle.

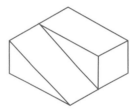

Which solid can be paired with it to make a cube?

A 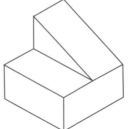      B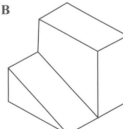

C 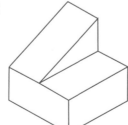      D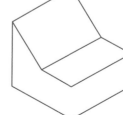

**5** Carrots are a source of important micronutrients that keep eyes healthy. If you eat carrots, you'll always have good eyesight.

Which one of these statements, if true, most **weakens** the above argument?

A Some eye diseases cannot be prevented by eating carrots.

B Exercise, wear sunglasses and eat a nutritious diet that includes carrots to help maintain eye health.

C Smoking cigarettes is very bad for eye health.

D Eighty per cent of vision impairment conditions can be treated or cured.

**6** Three friends decide to plant a fruit tree in the house that they share. They will only plant one tree.

Rachel only likes grapefruit, peaches and cherries. Micaela only likes grapefruit, mangoes and peaches. Brad likes all fruit except for grapefruit.

Which tree should they plant so that all three friends can eat the fruit from the tree?

A grapefruit

B peach

C cherry

D mango

**7** A father went outside and found his four children standing around a paint tin that had spilled paint all over the veranda. He asked who did it. They gave the following replies.

**Rocco:** 'It wasn't me.'

**Peter:** 'Katy did it.'

**Katy:** 'It wasn't me. It was Peter or Charles.'

**Charles:** 'I didn't do it. Peter did.'

If only one of the children is lying, who knocked over the paint tin?

A Rocco

B Peter

C Katy

D Charles

**8** A cat is the most common pet in Switzerland. Swiss people love their pet cats so much that many apartment buildings in Swiss cities have external cat ladders or ramps allowing cats to come and go as they please from their home unit balconies or windows. The cat has its freedom and the pet owner does not have to worry about being home to let the cat out or in.

Which statement best expresses the main idea of the text?

A A cat is the most common pet in Switzerland.

B Swiss people love their cats and install pet ladders so cats can come and go as they please.

C Cat ladders or ramps allow cats to come and go as they please from their home unit balconies or windows.

D In Switzerland cats have freedom and the pet owner does not have to worry about being home to let their pet cat out or in.

**9**
> If an item is inflammable, it means it can catch fire and burn very easily. If something is nonflammable, it means it does not readily catch on fire.
>
> To help keep children safer, nightwear for children in sizes 00 to 14 has to be labelled according to how flammable it is.

**Yassi:** 'When choosing children's pyjamas, you need to check the fire-hazard label to make sure the fabric is not nonflammable material.'

**Rhiannon:** 'Regardless of their clothing being nonflammable or not, it's best if children stay well away from heaters, candles or open fires. All fabrics will burn.'

If the information in the box is true, whose reasoning is incorrect?

A Yassi only

B Rhiannon only

C Both Yassi and Rhiannon

D Neither Yassi nor Rhiannon

**10** The weekly maths quiz consists of 10 questions. The results of three students for the first four weeks of the term are shown in the graph below.

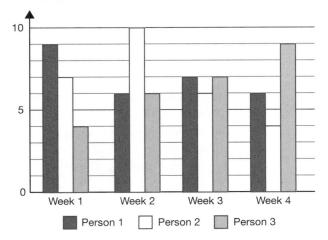

The difference between Cooper's best mark and his worst mark was the largest.

Kyle was the only student to get the same mark in two different weeks.

How many total marks did Maddie, the other student, score in her final two tests?

**A** 10 **B** 13 **C** 16 **D** 19

**11** A meat-eating diet is bad for the planet because livestock produces methane, which is a greenhouse gas that contributes to climate change. Growing meat also uses more water than growing meat alternatives such as beans, meaning that eating meat is unsustainable.

Our school has implemented a meat-free canteen policy. We began with meat-free Fridays only but now we have a fully meat-free canteen every day of the week. The canteen serves all our favourite foods but uses alternatives to meat. It's healthier for us too.

Which of these statements, if true, most **strengthens** the above argument?

**A** Using meat alternatives helps protect habitats from animal farming.

**B** The canteen makes a really good vegan spaghetti bolognaise.

**C** The school is influencing other schools to try a meat-free canteen.

**D** Students have been very supportive of the meat-free canteen.

**12**

**Kaliah:** 'Mum's new friend from work is coming for dinner tonight. We're going to make a vegan Thai red curry with rice. '

**Marco:** 'Your mum's new friend must be vegan.'

Which assumption has Marco made?

**A** When you invite someone to dinner you ask them what food they like to eat.

**B** Kaliah and her mother like Thai food.

**C** You cook vegan food only if the guest is vegan.

**D** Kaliah's mother must be vegan.

**13** In golf competitions the winner is the person who has the fewest shots after four rounds of a golf course. The results after the first two rounds are shown below.

| Name | 1st round | 2nd round |
|---|---|---|
| Ernie | 75 | 62 |
| Carrie | 73 | 63 |
| Greg | 68 | 71 |
| Minjee | 63 | 72 |
| Rory | 68 | 68 |
| Patty | 70 | 65 |
| Babe | 70 | 64 |

After the first round Minjee is in the lead (winning). Who is in the lead after the second round?

**A** Ernie **B** Minjee **C** Rory **D** Babe

☞ **Answers and explanations on pages 77–79**

**14** If Nonna can't get an urgent appointment to see her own doctor in his office, she can book a house call from an after-hours doctor who will come to her home. Alternatively she can go to an after-hours clinic to see a doctor. These clinics open at 6 pm but don't take appointments.

Which of the following statements is **not** possible?

**A** Nonna made an appointment with the after-hours doctor.

**B** Nonna made an appointment with the after-hours clinic.

**C** Nonna could get an appointment with her usual doctor.

**D** Nonna had a doctor visit her at home after hours.

**15** Helen, Trish, Pamela and Dawn competed in a swimming race.

Helen finished after Dawn but before Pamela.

Dawn finished before Trish.

What is **not** possible?

**A** Dawn finished in second place.

**B** Helen finished in third place.

**C** Helen finished in second place.

**D** Pamela finished in fourth place.

**1** Three friends are sitting at the table shown.

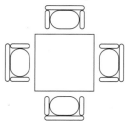

Toby is sitting opposite Bobby and Connor is sitting next to Toby.

What must be true?

**A** Bobby is sitting opposite the empty seat.

**B** Connor is sitting next to the empty seat.

**C** Toby is sitting on Connor's left.

**D** Bobby is sitting next to Connor.

**2** The Superb lyrebird does a great job helping the environment. It is a major earth mover. It tills and scratches at the soil and uses its powerful feet to move the soil behind it as it scratches. Each Superb lyrebird can move the equivalent of eleven dump trucks a year. In this way lyrebirds aerate the soil, spread leaf litter, and make grooves and channels in the soil for other species to use.

Which statement best expresses the main idea in the text?

**A** The Superb lyrebird aerates the soil, spreads leaf litter, and makes grooves and channels in the soil for other species to use.

**B** The Superb lyrebird uses its powerful feet to move the soil, aerating it and helping the environment.

**C** The Superb lyrebird is a major earth mover.

**D** The Superb lyrebird does a great job helping the environment.

**3** A pizza shop cuts its pizzas into four slices. Seven friends buy five pizzas: a Supreme, a Hawaiian, a Margherita and two Vegetarians.

If the friends share all the slices as evenly as they can, what **must** be true?

**A** Someone gets 2 slices of the same type of pizza.

**B** No one gets 3 slices of pizza.

**C** No one gets 2 slices of pizza.

**D** Someone will get 4 slices of pizza.

**4** Three friends are discussing the foods they choose when they attend their bowls club buffet nights. Flynn always has soup first then he picks seafood, such as prawns and oysters, and then the roast meat with baked veggies. For dessert he likes pavlova. Chandra chooses soup and garlic bread, then the roast with baked vegetables and some salad, then the chocolate fountain for dessert. Aaron likes pizza and pasta as well as the roast. For dessert he likes the chocolate fountain.

Which foods does Chandra choose from a buffet that neither Flynn nor Aaron chooses?

**A** prawns, oysters and pizza

**B** pavlova and salad

**C** salad and garlic bread

**D** garlic bread and pizza

**5** A restaurant serves four meals throughout the day.

| Breakfast | is from 9 am to 12 noon. |
| Lunch | is from 12 noon to 3 pm. |
| Tea | is from 3 pm to 6 pm. |
| Dinner | is from 6 pm to 9 pm. |

Four friends are planning to eat at the restaurant together.

The following shows when each person is available to go to the restaurant.

| Name | 9 am | | 12 noon | | 3 pm | | 6 pm | |
|------|------|---|---------|---|------|---|------|---|
| Glenn | ▨ | | ▨ | | ▨ | | | ▨ |
| Nihan | | | | | ▨ | ▨ | | |
| Vinesh | | ▨ | | | | | | |
| David | | | | | | | | |

☐ Available to eat     ▨ Not available

Which meal are the friends **not** able to eat together?

**A** breakfast          **B** lunch

**C** tea               **D** dinner

**6** Four buildings are on a city block, surrounded by four streets.

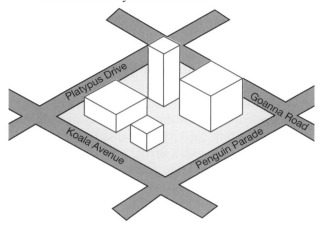

Which is **not** a possible side view of the block from one of the streets?

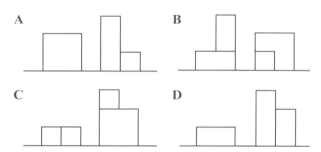

A      B

C      D

**7** **Yi Min:** 'Whenever I leave Jaffa inside when I go out she gets up to mischief such as gnawing on the pantry cupboard door to get to where her treats are stored. If I leave her outside, she barks and annoys the neighbours. One of my neighbours is a nurse who often works at night and needs to sleep during the day. It upsets her when she can't get enough sleep.'

**Philippe:** 'Yi Min's neighbour, the nurse, was upset on Tuesday night. Jaffa must have been left outside to bark all day on Tuesday.'

**Emily:** 'If Jaffa is left outside tomorrow and barks all day, then the nurse will not get any sleep and will be upset.'

If the information in the box is true, whose reasoning is correct?

**A** Philippe only
**B** Emily only
**C** Both Philippe and Emily
**D** Neither Philippe nor Emily

**8** Look at the square below.

If you have the piece shown, which option shows the three other pieces that will complete the square?

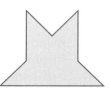

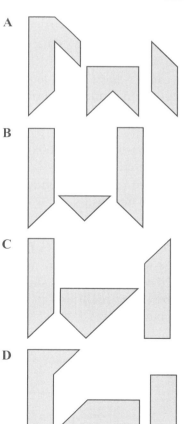

A

B

C

D

**9** Sasha and Dane are in the vegetable garden.

**Sasha:** 'Mum asked me to pick her some coriander. She says not to confuse it for flat-leafed parsley. The coriander has more rounded, lacy-looking leaves and has a stronger smell than parsley if you rub the leaves between your fingers to check the aromas.'

**Dane:** 'Here's a green-leafed herb with a strong smell. It must be the coriander.'

Which one of the following sentences shows the mistake Dane has made?

**A** Just because it has a green leaf and smells does not mean it must be coriander.

**B** It's easy to confuse coriander with flat-leafed parsley.

**C** Coriander has more lacy-looking leaves than flat-leafed parsley.

**D** Dane did not rub the coriander leaves between his fingers.

**10** Ian is paving an outdoor area. He starts paving at 7:30 am and wants to finish paving before he stops for lunch. The area he is paving is 20 square metres as shown below. Each square metre requires 4 pavers and Ian can lay 16 pavers every hour.

The diagram shows the outdoor area after he lays the first 4 pavers.

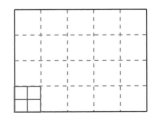

1 square metre

At what time will Ian be able to stop for lunch?

**A** 11:30 am      **B** 12:00 pm

**C** 12:30 pm      **D** 1:00 pm

**11** Rose, Louis and Young-ro all bought air fryers at the same time and have been discussing their favourite items to cook. Rose likes to cook potatoes, pumpkin, parsnips, capsicum and mushrooms. Louis likes to use his air fryer for hash browns, sausage rolls and leftover pizza slices, as well as for potato and pumpkin. Young-ro cooks zucchini chips, hash browns, mushrooms and muffins.

Which of the following does Rose cook in her air fryer that neither Louis nor Young-ro cooks?

**A** mushrooms and zucchini

**B** capsicum and mushrooms

**C** parsnips and capsicum

**D** potatoes and pumpkin

**12** Families have special words they use when together that they know the meanings of. My little brother calls an ambulance an 'ambliance'; hospital is a 'hostabull'; Grandpa is 'Oompah'; Grandma is 'Leelu'; our dog is Plod Plod even though his name is Caesar, which sounds nothing like Plod Plod. He calls our baby sister Ali-oops, thinking that is her real name. Her name is Ali but when Dad swings her high and pretends to drop her he calls out 'Ali-oops!' Families establish special bonds through using their secret language.

Which of the following is the main idea of the text?

**A** Families have special words they use when together that they know the meanings of.

**B** The writer's family uses special words that make sense to them but not to anyone else.

**C** The writer's younger brother and sister have invented a language of their own.

**D** Families establish special bonds through using their secret language.

☞ **Answers and explanations on pages 79–80**

**13** The first four steps in a pattern are shown.

What is the next step in the pattern?

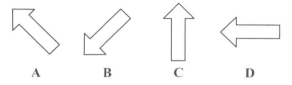

|  A  |  B  |  C  |  D  |

**14** Timo and Jerome have a secret way of writing to each other. They send a message that is hidden using a cipher. They also send with it three messages that make no sense. This is to confuse any siblings that might come across the message. They use one of the ciphers below to hide their message.

Cipher 1: Replace each letter with the next letter in the alphabet.

Cipher 2: Replace each letter with the previous letter in the alphabet.

For example, using cipher 1 the word HELLO would be written as IFMMP. Using cipher 2 the word HELLO would be written as GDKKN.

Timo sent four messages to Jerome. Which one is the real message?

**A** HGSIUMGUUTNDJJ

**B** CSJOHBGPPUCBMM

**C** INFFXGTHHEANND

**D** HPPQCDHTHNUUST

**15** Huan's class was asked to vote on the theme for a whole-class mural to be painted on the side of the library. Everyone had to vote for two themes. The choices were: Under the Sea, Tropical Rainforest or Desert Habitat. Twenty-eight students voted. Every theme got at least one vote.

Knowing **one** of the following would allow us to know the result of the vote. Which one is it?

**A** Every student voted for either Under the Sea or Desert Habitat, or both.

**B** The Tropical Rainforest was one of the two more popular votes.

**C** No student voted for both Tropical Rainforest and Under the Sea.

**D** Under the Sea only got eight votes.

**1** Three solids are placed on top of each other to create an object. The side view is shown below.

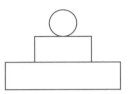

Which of the following is **not** a possible top view of the pile?

 A

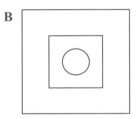 B

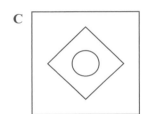 C

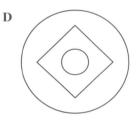 D

**2**

**Sheridan:** 'I've found a great new recipe using quinoa!'

**Bryan:** 'You must love quinoa.'

Which assumption has Bryan made?

A People search for recipes that use ingredients they love.

B Sheridan has searched for a quinoa recipe.

C Sheridan likes to try out new recipes.

D Sheridan enjoys cooking.

**3** Dog shows are held around Australia each year. Competitions are held for different breeds and classes. Judges examine aspects of each dog's physical appearance, coat condition and gait.

**Kashif:** 'Eric's English cocker spaniel Barney won the Best in Breed category last year. He's sure to win that category again this year and then he will compete against all the other Best in Breed winners for the title of Best in Show.'

**Monique:** 'I doubt Bindi's Labrador Reggie will win Best in Show but she might win the Best in Breed category. Labradors are lovely dogs and they are a very popular breed but rarely win Best in Show so I am not confident for Monique this year.'

If the information in the box is true, whose reasoning is correct?

A Kashif only

B Monique only

C Both Kashif and Monique

D Neither Kashif nor Monique

**4**

Which pair of solids below **cannot** be used together to make the solid above? They may be rotated and flipped.

A

B

C

D

**5** Anastasia said: 'My stepdad hesitates about making donations to charity because he worries that a large portion of his donated money will be used on the charity's administration costs. Some people do not donate to charities at all because of these concerns.'

Which one of these statements, if true, most **weakens** Anastasia's stepdad's argument?

**A** Some people donate such poor-quality items to charity that charities have to pay for the rubbish to be removed.

**B** Running a charity costs money and these costs are not a waste of money.

**C** Before you donate money to a charity you can ask what percentage of your money will actually go to the cause you want to support.

**D** Charities rely on the goodwill of people who make donations.

**6** Helga has a lemon tree, an orange tree and a grapefruit tree in her backyard. The amount of fruit that each tree has produced over the last four years is shown in the graph.

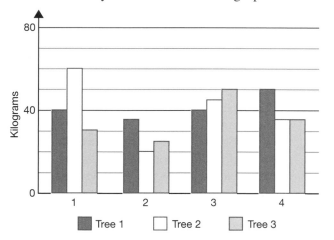

- The lemon tree produced the most fruit over the four years.
- The orange tree produced the same amount of fruit in years 1 and 2 as it did in years 3 and 4.

How many kilograms of fruit did the grapefruit tree produce in its second-best year?

**A** 45 kg
**B** 40 kg
**C** 35 kg
**D** 30 kg

**7** The Paraan family wanted to get a pet but not everyone liked the same animals. They had to choose from a dog, a cat, a rabbit, a turtle and a bird.

Ray liked all animals except rabbits. Patrick liked all animals except birds. Geri liked birds, rabbits and cats but no other animals. Adrian loved turtles the best but likes all animals.

What pet should the family get to keep everyone happy?

**A** dog
**B** cat
**C** turtle
**D** bird

**8** When Shintaro was learning his lines as one of the main characters in the school play his teacher told him: 'To have even a chance of learning your lines perfectly by the time you have to perform for an audience, you must have at least fifteen hours of practice.'

If Shintaro's teacher is correct, which one of these statements will be true?

**A** Actors in the play who have had fifteen or more hours of practice will not be able to learn their lines in time.

**B** All of the main character actors in the play who had more than fifteen hours of practice will have difficulty learning their lines in time.

**C** None of the main character actors who have had less than fifteen hours of practice will have learnt their lines in time.

**D** Only the actors who have had less than fifteen hours of practice will have learned their lines in time.

**9** Birds need a balanced diet of seeds, insects, nectar and fruit. Feeding them human food has negative consequences for their health. Feeding birds bread can cause sickness and deformities in baby birds because bread has too much salt and too many calories for birds. Feeding birds raw meat is also bad for their health because raw meat does not contain the calcium and phosphorus they need for healthy bones.

Which statement below best expresses the main idea in the text?

**A** Birds need a balanced diet of seeds, insects, nectar and fruit.

**B** Birds can usually get enough natural food for their good health.

**C** Please do not feed the birds.

**D** Feeding birds human food has negative consequences for their health.

**10** Over the period of 1 hour, James took note of how many birds used the birdbath in his backyard. He noticed four species of bird use his birdbath and drew the following graph to show how many of each there were. Each rectangle in the graph represents the same number of birds.

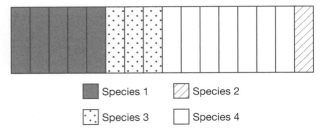

Species 1  Species 2
Species 3  Species 4

There were three times as many pigeons as king parrots.

There were 6 more galahs than there were rosellas.

How many rosellas used James's birdbath in the hour?

**A** 5
**B** 7
**C** 15
**D** 21

**11** A sloth is a lethargic, slow-moving, Central- and South-American tree-dwelling mammal. Sloths spend most of their days sleeping in the treetops. On average an adult sloth does not even travel 40 metres in a day.

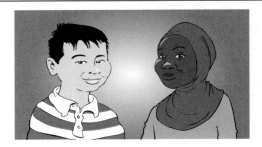

**Joshua:** 'My mum calls Uncle Doug a sloth. I don't think she means he likes to sleep in the treetops!'

**Christina:** 'I think she means your Uncle Doug doesn't do much. She probably thinks he's lazy or sleepy.'

If the information in the box is true, whose reasoning is correct?

**A** Joshua only
**B** Christina only
**C** Both Joshua and Christina
**D** Neither Joshua nor Christina

**12** Three friends who live in Sydney are comparing where in Australia they have travelled for holidays over their lifetimes. Lai has travelled to Canberra, the Snowy Mountains, Dubbo Zoo, Orange, Parkes, Bathurst, Nambucca Heads, Byron Bay and Coffs Harbour. Keeley has travelled to Byron Bay, Coffs Harbour, Nambucca Heads, Dorrigo, Hawks Nest, Port Macquarie, Lismore and the Central Coast. Tallulah has travelled to Bateman's Bay, Canberra, Kiama, Hawks Nest, Port Macquarie, Wollongong and the Central Coast.

Where has Keeley travelled to on holidays that neither Lai nor Tallulah has travelled to?

**A** Kiama and Hawks Nest
**B** the Snowy Mountains and Canberra
**C** Byron Bay and Wollongong
**D** Lismore and Dorrigo

**13** Lauren records how long each cat sleeps over the weekend to find the laziest cat.

| Cat | Hours asleep Saturday | Hours asleep Sunday |
|---|---|---|
| Ruby | 13 | 10 |
| Theo | 12 | 19 |
| Delilah | 18 | 15 |
| Pepe | 16 | |

One number is missing from the table. Lauren found that Pepe is the laziest cat.

What must be true?

A Pepe slept for more than 17 hours on Sunday.

B Pepe slept for more than 18 hours on Sunday.

C Pepe slept more than Theo on Sunday

D Pepe slept for less than 20 hours on Sunday.

**14** **Tristan:** 'I'm going to buy a lemon tree to plant in my backyard. It should give me lots of lemons.'

**Suhana:** 'You must eat a lot of lemons.'

Which assumption has Suhana made?

A Anyone who likes to eat lemons grows lemons.

B Anyone can grow a lot of lemons.

C Anyone who chooses to grow lemons must like to eat lemons.

D To eat a lot of lemons you must know how to grow them yourself.

**15** Gail knits four jumpers for her friends. She gives the second-largest jumper to John. The green jumper, which is not the smallest, she gives to Hannah. Kristine is given the yellow jumper which is smaller than William's. The red jumper is smaller than the blue jumper.

What colour is the smallest jumper?

A green

B yellow

C red

D blue

**1** Three friends are sitting at the table shown below.

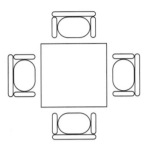

Nicola is not sitting opposite Fleur but Nicola is sitting opposite Cora.

What **cannot** be true?

A Fleur is sitting opposite the empty chair.

B Fleur is sitting opposite Cora.

C Fleur is sitting on Cora's left.

D Fleur is sitting on Cora's right.

**2** Malaria is a serious disease in some parts of the world. Every year millions of people get malaria and many die from it. Mostly these are children. Malaria is spread by female mosquito bite. It can be easily prevented by controlling mosquitoes with insecticide or by providing people with bed nets that have been treated with insecticides.

If the information above is true, which statement best supports the argument?

A Avoid outdoor activities between dusk and dawn when mosquitoes are most active.

B Medications to treat malaria are not readily available to people in poorer countries.

C Symptoms of malaria include fever, headache and nausea.

D World Malaria Day aims to control and eradicate malaria worldwide.

**3** In a drawstring bag there are 15 marbles. Three are black, 4 are blue and 8 are yellow. How many marbles must Jericho pull out of the bag to be certain of getting at least 2 yellow marbles?

A 9     B 8     C 5     D 4

**4** **Ms Peacock:** 'All 26 students in my class were asked to bring a photo of one of their pets to display on the back wall of the classroom today. I know everyone has a pet. I also know eight children in the class have dogs but I only saw five photos of dogs on the back wall. The other three students who have dogs must have forgotten to bring their photos.'

Which one of the following sentences shows the mistake Ms Peacock has made?

A Some students might not have had a photo of their dog to bring.

B All dog owners would have chosen to bring a dog photo rather than a photo of another pet.

C Eight children might not own dogs.

D Ms Peacock did not count the photos on display to check if there were 26.

**5** Three buildings are on a city block, surrounded by four streets.

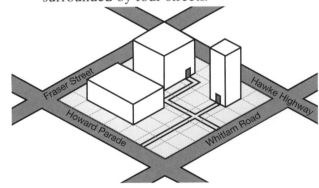

Which is **not** a possible side view of the block from one of the streets?

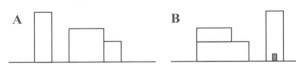

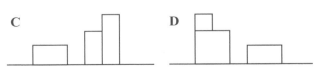

**6** Jason asked his friends who ate his leftover spaghetti. They gave the following replies.

**Kris:** 'Not me, I don't like spaghetti.'

**Yusuf:** 'I didn't eat it. Lily did.'

**Lily:** 'I saw Kris eat it.'

If only one of the friends is lying, who ate the spaghetti?

A Kris

B Yusuf

C Lily

D Not enough information

**7** Around ten people a year die due to lightning strikes in Australia. The northwest coast of Australia has the most lightning strikes of anywhere in Australia. A lightning strike can kill or injure a person so it's best to avoid behaviour that puts you at risk of being struck by lightning.

Which of the following sentences best expresses the main idea of the above argument?

A Stay away from open fields, hilltops or mountain tops during a lightning storm.

B A lightning strike can kill or injure a person so avoid risky behaviour.

C The northwest coast of Australia has a lot of lightning strikes.

D If you are caught outdoors, immediately seek a safe place to shelter.

**8** There are two types of puzzle piece.

Glenn must use four pieces to create a picture. He can use as many of each of the pieces as he wants. For example, he can use four of the pieces on the right and none of the pieces on the left.

Which of the following pictures can Glenn **not** create?

A 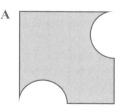          B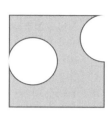

C 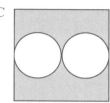          D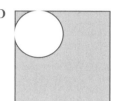

**9**

**Mitchell:** 'Charlie is always practising his guitar. He practises for hours every day.'

**Nasin:** 'He must be hopeless.'

What is Nasin's assumption?

A Only people who are hopeless practise as much as Charlie.

B Charlie must be a great player after so much practice.

C Practice is important for guitarists.

D Charlie must really enjoy practising.

**10** The first, second, third and fifth steps of a pattern are shown. The fourth step is missing.

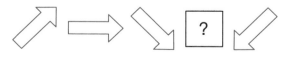

What shape shows the fourth step?

A          B          C          D

11. The vet said our cat is overweight and it's bad for his health. We have to help Dexter get down to a healthier weight. The vet has given us some tips. One tip is to add water to his food so that he thinks he's eating the same amount of food and will feel full. Another tip is to use a treat ball so he has to work for his food. This will give Dexter more exercise than he usually gets.

Which one of these statements, if true, best supports the vet's claims?

A The vet said we've been feeding our cat too much high-carb food.

B Our cat's name is Dexter but we've been calling him Mr Chubby.

C The vet said being overweight can lead to diseases such as diabetes.

D Our cat mostly sleeps and does not like to move around very much.

12. Carlos delivers menus for a restaurant into the letterboxes of houses. He can deliver to 40 houses in one hour. If Carlos works from 3:30 pm when he finishes school until 7:00 pm, but has a 15-minute break at 5:00 pm, how many menus does he deliver?

A 115

B 120

C 130

D 155

13. **Jack:** 'Cassie never washes her car.'

**Paris:** 'Cassie doesn't care if her car is dirty.'

What assumption has Paris made?

A Cassie doesn't enjoy washing her car.

B Cassie doesn't have time to wash her car.

C If someone's car is dirty, it's because they don't care about it being dirty.

D If you cared about your car being dirty, you'd wash it.

14. Malcolm sent a Christmas message to his friend Priya but used a special cipher so no-one else could read it. He replaced each letter with the third letter after it.

For example, A is replaced by D and B is replaced by E. When he reached the end of the alphabet, he just started again. So X is replaced by A and Y is replaced by B.

HELLO would be written as KHOOR.

In his message, Malcolm made a mistake. Which word has the mistake?

A SXGGKPI

B PHUUB

C GHDU

D SUHVHQW

15. The European honey bee, the European Bumble bee, the South African carder bee, the Mediterranean Emerald Furrow bee and the Asian honey bee are not native Australian bees. The European honey bee is the most common bee in Australia. It was introduced to Australia in 1822 by the early colonists to make honey. Introduced bees compete with native bees for food and nesting sites. Some Australian native flowers can only be pollinated by native Australian bees and so those native plants could become endangered if we don't look after our native bees.

On the basis of this information, which one of the following statements **cannot** be true?

A Introduced bees and native bees eat the same food.

B Early colonists enjoyed honey.

C Introduced species of bee are a threat to native bees and native plants.

D Native bees are the most common bees in Australia.

## IDENTIFYING THE MAIN IDEA

Page 1

1 **B is correct.** The main idea is that the Greenhill Botanic Gardens are now open. The rest of the text supports this idea with more information about why the gardens had been closed and what you can do in the gardens once again.

**A is incorrect.** This is supporting information for the main idea, explaining why the gardens had been closed.

**C is incorrect.** This information is not in the text so cannot be the main idea.

**D is incorrect.** This is supporting information for the main idea.

2 **A is correct.** The main idea is that cats are afraid of cucumbers. This is stated in the opening sentence and reinforced in the conclusion. The rest of the text gives supporting information about why cats are afraid of cucumbers.

**B is incorrect.** This is supporting information for the main idea.

**C is incorrect.** This information is not in the text so cannot be the main idea.

**D is incorrect.** The text says 'Even if a cat has not seen a snake in their life' not that they never see them. Therefore this is not in the text and cannot be the main idea.

## IDENTIFYING A CONCLUSION THAT MUST BE TRUE

Page 2

1 **C is correct.** According to Mr Lin if a student has not read at least 20 books, they do not have a chance of receiving a prize. Therefore none of the students who have read less than 20 books will receive a prize. So this statement must be true.

**A is incorrect.** According to Mr Lin, having read 20 books gives a student only a **chance** of receiving a prize. It does not guarantee a prize.

**B is incorrect.** Mr Lin says students must have read **at least** 20 books, not **less than** 20 books.

**D is incorrect.** Mr Lin says students **must** have read at least 20 books so this statement cannot be true.

2 **D is correct.** Riding a motorbike and gardening are both included in the list of activities Grandma would like to do but neither Dad nor Isla mentions either one.

**A is incorrect.** Grandma wants to go on a picnic and ride a motorbike but Isla would also like to go on a picnic.

**B is incorrect.** Grandma wants to do some gardening and go on a bushwalk but Isla would also like to go on a bushwalk.

**C is incorrect.** Grandma does not want to play golf or visit Uncle Frank.

## IDENTIFYING A CONCLUSION THAT IS NOT POSSIBLE

Page 3

1 **C is correct.** It cannot be true that Jeannie did not go to school by car on Tuesday. She goes to school by car on Tuesday when her father drives her because she has swimming before school.

**A is incorrect.** It could be true that Jeannie walked to school on Monday with Adam and Lana.

**B is incorrect.** It could be true that Adam and Lana walked to school on Tuesday without Jeannie because Jeannie's father drives her on Tuesdays.

**D is incorrect.** It could be true that Jeannie walked to school on Friday.

2 **D is correct.** The store that gave customers a free case for every guitar purchased did not have stock so it cannot be true that Colin took the guitar home immediately.

**A is incorrect.** One of the stores offered five free guitar lessons with every guitar purchased but there was a month's wait.

**B is incorrect.** It could be true that Colin decides not to buy a guitar at this time.

**C is incorrect.** This could be true. The third store had stock and the guitar was the same price but there was no free bonus case with purchase.

### IDENTIFYING **EVIDENCE THAT LEADS TO A CONCLUSION**    Page 4

1   **D is correct.** Knowing that no-one voted for both Japanese and Thai tells you that everyone voted for Japanese and Chinese, or Thai and Chinese. That means everyone voted for Chinese and it was therefore the kind of food eaten on Saturday night.

**A is incorrect.** The information only tells you that Thai did not win. It does not tell you which food won.

**B is incorrect.** This information only tells you that Japanese **might** have won. It does not tell you which food definitely won.

**C is incorrect.** This information does not allow you to know the result of the vote. It only tells you the result was either Thai food or Chinese food.

2   **C is correct.** Knowing that no-one voted for both Sweet Tooth Smoothies and Smoothie Paradise tells you everyone voted for Sweet Tooth Smoothies and Secret Garden Smoothies, or Smoothie Paradise and Secret Garden Smoothies. This means everyone used one of their votes to vote for Secret Garden Smoothies and it was therefore chosen as the name of the stall.

**A is incorrect.** This information does not allow you to know the result of the vote. It only tells you the result was either Smoothie Paradise or Secret Garden Smoothies.

**B is incorrect.** This information only tells you Sweet Tooth Smoothies **could** have won. It does not tell you which name definitely won.

**D is incorrect.** This information only tells you Smoothie Paradise did not win. It does not tell you which name won.

### DENTIFYING **AN ASSUMPTION**    Page 5

1   **B is correct.** For the conclusion to hold, it must be assumed that building a new car park is a good thing. (The Council wants to build a new car park + building a new car park is a good thing means therefore we must support the proposal to build a new car park.)

**A is incorrect.** This is the evidence the writer has used to support the conclusion.

**C is incorrect.** This is the conclusion the writer has drawn, based on the assumption that building a new car park is a good thing.

**D is incorrect.** This assumption would not support the conclusion. (The Council wants to build a new car park + we should not build a new car park does not mean therefore we must support the proposal to build a new car park.)

2   **A is correct.** Violet's conclusion is that they should sit up front. She based this conclusion on the evidence that Harvey says it's scarier at the front of the cars. So, for her conclusion to hold, it must be assumed that Harvey wants to be scared. (Harvey says it's scarier at the front of the cars + Harvey wants to be scared means therefore they should sit up front.)

**B is incorrect.** This would not support the conclusion that they should sit up front.

**C is incorrect.** This is Violet's conclusion.

**D is incorrect.** This is the evidence Violet has used to draw her conclusion.

### IDENTIFYING **CORRECT REASONING**    Page 6

1   **A is correct.** The information tells you only aged-care residents who have a family member to sign them out and vouch for their safety will be allowed out of the facility this weekend. Therefore Lina's reasoning is correct. Eric will not be allowed out because he does not have any family member to sign him out.

**B is incorrect.** Simon is wrong to state that Pauline will be allowed out because we don't know if further government lockdowns will occur.

**C is incorrect.** Lina is correct but Simon is not so this option is incorrect.

**D is incorrect.** Lina is correct so this option is incorrect.

2   **A is correct.** Brooke is correct to reason that if the battery has not been beeping, then you can tell it still has a charge.

**B is incorrect.** Amy is incorrect to assert that if the battery isn't beeping, there's no need to replace it. She has not accounted for the fact the battery might not be beeping because it has run out of charge. The battery could have been beeping but stopped beeping because it is dead.

**C is incorrect.** Amy is not correct so this option is incorrect.

**D is incorrect.** Brooke is correct so this option is incorrect.

## IDENTIFYING FLAWED REASONING
Page 8

1 **A is correct.** Lachlan's mistake is that because he can't find plain biscuits in a red wrapper he thinks Nana has made a mistake about the wrapper colour.

**B is incorrect.** Elsa does not know the brand but this is not the mistake Lachlan has made.

**C is incorrect.** This would not be true, as Nana specifically wants her favourite biscuits in the red wrapper. This is also not the mistake Lachlan has made.

**D is incorrect.** This could be true. The store Elsa and Lachlan are looking in might not be the store where Nana gets her biscuits. However, this statement is not the mistake Lachlan has made when he declares that the biscuits in the brown wrapper are the biscuits Nana wants and that Nana must have made a mistake with the colour.

2 **D is correct.** Mr Dreyfus's mistake is that he seems to have assumed that every grandparent will attend and if a student has no grandparents attending, then those grandparents must not be alive. He has not considered other reasons for grandparents not to attend. Grandparents might not have replied yet. Some grandparents might live a long way from the school and be unable to attend for travel reasons, might not have access to transport or may be in poor health.

**A and B are incorrect.** These suggestions are irrelevant.

**C is incorrect.** This could be true but it's not the mistake Mr Dreyfus has made.

## IDENTIFYING ADDITIONAL EVIDENCE TO STRENGTHEN A CLAIM
Page 9

1 **D is correct.** The council claims that the community needs to remain vigilant about mosquitoes, supporting this claim with information about why people need to be vigilant and what they can do. The statement that mosquito numbers are higher than usual best supports this claim.

**A and C are incorrect.** This statement is not relevant to the claim that the community needs to remain vigilant.

**B is incorrect.** This statement could possibly support the claim but does not best support it.

2 **C is correct.** The statement that stroking a dog can lower blood pressure and ease anxiety best supports the claim that having a bond with animals improves the quality of life for humans.

**A is incorrect.** This statement does not support the claim that having a bond with an animal improves a person's quality of life.

**B is incorrect.** This statement could help support a claim about the benefits of therapy dogs but does not best support the volunteer's claim.

**D is incorrect.** This statement might be the purpose of the interview but is not relevant to the volunteer's claim.

## IDENTIFYING ADDITIONAL EVIDENCE TO WEAKEN AN ARGUMENT
Page 10

1 **A is correct.** The argument is that the swimming carnival is preferred to the athletics carnival because of the weather at the times when the carnivals are usually held. March is usually warm for swimming and August is usually windy and unpleasant for athletics. The statement that the swimming carnival is sometimes held in a cooler month means the weather will be cooler and will make the swimming carnival likely to be less popular. This weakens the argument.

**B is incorrect.** February is warmer than March so the swimming carnival will remain more popular.

**C and D are incorrect.** These statements are irrelevant to the argument.

2   **B is correct.** The argument is that the gym will become busier as more people in the building turn 65 and retire from work over the next five years. The statement that there is a trend for people to continue working past the age of 65 suggests that the predicted increase in gym use won't happen. This statement weakens the argument by undermining it or contradicting it.

**The other options are incorrect.** These statements are irrelevant to the argument.

## SHARING ITEMS OUT EVENLY   Page 11

1   **D is correct.** Jasmin could pull a red lolly out first but it is not certain. You need to work out the number she needs to pull out to be certain of a red lolly.

If Jasmin pulled out all the brown and all the green lollies first, she would pull out 9 lollies that are not red as 2 brown + 7 green = 9 total. Then there would be only red lollies left in the bag. The tenth lolly she would pull out **must** be a red lolly.

To be **certain** of getting a red lolly, Jasmin must pull 10 lollies out of the bag.

2   **C is correct.** This is a division question. 15 cats shared between 6 cages gives 2 cats per cage and a remainder of 3 cats. The remaining 3 cats will be shared between 3 cages that already have 2 cats in them. There will be 3 cages with 3 cats and 3 cages with 2 cats.

## CALCULATIONS INVOLVING TIME   Page 12

1   **B is correct.** How long is Lee working? There are 4 hours between 11 am and 3 pm but she breaks for half an hour. So she works for $3\frac{1}{2}$ hours (3.5 hours or 3 hours 30 minutes).

How many mugs can she make in an hour? One mug in 10 minutes means 2 mugs in 20 minutes. This means 6 mugs in 60 minutes, which is one hour. She makes 6 mugs every hour.

In 3 hours she makes $3 \times 6 = 18$ mugs. In half an hour she makes 3 mugs. In 3 and a half hours she makes $18 + 3 = 21$ mugs.

  6 mugs per hour × 3.5 hours = 21 mugs

2   **B is correct.** In this question, it is important to find out how Glenn will bowl. If he practises from 3:30 pm to 4:00 pm, that is 30 minutes. But he has a 10-minute break between 3:40 pm and 3:50 pm.

This means he bowls for 20 minutes.

If he bowls 3 balls in 1 minute, he will bowl 30 balls in 10 minutes, as $3 \times 10 = 30$. As he is bowling for 20 minutes, he will bowl 60 balls, as $2 \times 30 = 60$.

## USING A PROCESS OF ELIMINATION   Page 13

1   **B is correct.** By listing the sports and crossing them off as you read each piece of information you will get to the answer.

After Gina:
netball, basketball, tennis, soccer, ~~Aussie rules~~
After Andrew:
~~netball~~, basketball, tennis, soccer, ~~Aussie rules~~
After Kerry:
~~netball~~, basketball, ~~tennis~~, soccer, ~~Aussie rules~~
After Mike:
~~netball~~, basketball, ~~tennis~~, ~~soccer~~, ~~Aussie rules~~
Leaving you with basketball, the answer.

2   **D is correct.** By listing the flavours and crossing them off as you read the information, you can find the answer.

After Helena:
lime, rasp., mango, lemon, orange, ~~pine.~~, ~~cola~~
After Louisa:
~~lime~~, rasp., mango, ~~lemon~~, orange, ~~pine.~~, ~~cola~~
After Belle:
~~lime~~, ~~rasp.~~, mango, ~~lemon~~, ~~orange~~, ~~pine.~~, ~~cola~~
Leaving you with mango, the answer.

## FINDING HIDDEN INFORMATION   Page 14

1   **D is correct.** If Chiara is telling the truth, then she didn't do it. Tom is lying, so Jannie didn't break it. Walt is lying, so Tom didn't break it. This leaves Walt as the person who broke the statue.

2   **C is correct.** Cinda said that Harald lost it. Harald and Marius both say things that disagree with Cinda. This means if she is telling the truth, then Harald and Marius are lying.

Bernie is also lying if she is telling the truth as he says that Cinda lost the football. So if she is the only one telling the truth, then Harald lost the football.

If she is lying, then Harald and Marius must be telling the truth. As only one person is telling the truth, Cinda can't be lying.

## SOLVING 3D PUZZLES
Page 15

1 **A is correct.** Turn the original piece over in your head and see which piece it might fit with. Pretend you have stuck a stick through the side and turned it over. Focus on one section of the piece, maybe the sloped section. Where will this end up? Will this fit with any of the answers? The hidden edges that were on the top are shown with the dotted lines in the second diagram.

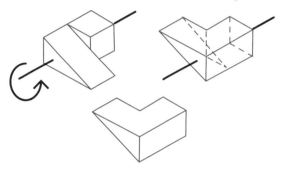

Here is the piece from A. The original piece, once turned over, fits perfectly to make a cube.

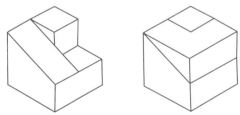

2 **D is correct.** Try turning each piece over in your head to see if it will fit on top of the piece that is given. Where will the sloped section be? Will it line up with the other sloped section?

When D is turned over and rotated, it fits to make a cube.

## VIEWING OBJECTS FROM DIFFERENT SIDES
Page 17

1 **C is correct.** The tallest building is visible from both sides. The large rectangle is the tall building. Any line across it is the top of one of the other buildings.

By counting the rows of windows, we can see that the building on the far left (5 rows) is more than halfway up the tallest building (8 rows). We cannot see the small building on the right as it is hidden, so there should be no line across at halfway. This rules out A and B. The second building from the left should be visible as it is taller than the first building. So we should see 2 lines across the tall rectangle. This rules out D.

2 **B is correct.** Pick a shape and try to judge everything based off that shape. A good shape to pick is the triangle as it points nicely at other shapes. In this question, if the triangle is in the bottom right corner, it should be pointing at the square above it. The circle should be next to it, and the hexagon should be in the opposite corner.

## READING TIMETABLES
Page 19

1 **D is correct.** The three teachers in the question (Mr White, Mrs Black and Mr Brown) must all be on break at the same time so they can have a meeting. So there needs to be a grey rectangle in the three teachers' rows at the same time (Miss Green and Mr Pink are irrelevant).

If they meet at 9 am, Mrs Black wouldn't be able to meet them as she is teaching at that time. Only Mr Brown is on break at 11 am so that is no good. None of them are on break at 12 noon, but all three are on break from 2 pm to 3 pm.

2 **D is correct.** Zeno is only at the camp Monday, Thursday and Friday. Geometry is not on Monday or Thursday, so Zeno must choose it on Friday. This means he must choose Infinity on Monday. So he only has Thursday left to fill with a subject. This means he can choose any other subject that is on a Thursday.

The Circle is not available on Thursday. Every other subject is available.

## QUESTIONS ABOUT GRAPHS
Page 21

**1 B is correct.** We need to work out two things to answer this question.

Which types of rectangle show which trees? How many trees does each little rectangle stand for?

The light purple must be waratahs as there are more of them than any other tree. There were half as many banksia as wattle, which means the dark purple is banksia which is 2 rectangles and the white is wattle, which has 4 rectangles. This means the spotted rectangles are for the bottlebrush. There are 3 of them.

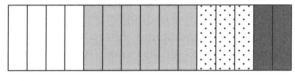

■ Banksia　⋰ Bottlebrush　▨ Waratah　□ Wattle

There are 15 rectangles altogether to stand for 60 trees. Each rectangle is 4 trees as 4 trees × 15 rectangles = 60 trees.

So there are 12 bottlebrush as 4 trees × 3 rectangles = 12 trees.

**2 A is correct.** We need to work out which pattern represents which student, then count up all of Esther's marks.

If Kira and Esther scored the same on a test, they must be the purple and spotted columns, as they scored 6 marks each on Wednesday. If Kira scored 10 in a test, she must be the spots, as the spots scored a 10 on Tuesday. Esther must be the purple.

Esther scored 6 + 4 + 6 + 5 = 21 marks over the four days.

## IDENTIFYING AND FOLLOWING A PATTERN
Page 22

**1 D is correct.** What is happening between each step of the pattern? What is happening to the crescent? What is happening to the lightning bolt?

The crescent is rotating by a quarter turn in the anti-clockwise direction. The lightning bolt is rotating in a clockwise direction.

We can rule out A and B following this pattern. Now we are left with two very similar answers in C and D. But C is not the same lightning bolt rotated. It is actually a reflection of the lightning bolt. So the correct answer is D.

**2 B is correct.** What is happening between each step of the pattern?

The arrow goes from the end of the row to the start and is turned upside down. The other two shapes stay the same, but just shift one space to the right. Does this happen again?

In the next step, the lightning bolt goes from the end of the row to the start and is turned upside down. The other shapes stay the same, but shift one space to the right.

So each step of the pattern moves the last shape to the front of the line and rotates it a half turn.

So the next step in the pattern should move the crescent to the front of the line and turn it upside down. The correct answer is B.

## SAMPLE TEST 1A Page 23

1 B 2 A 3 B 4 A 5 C 6 A 7 C 8 A 9 B
10 D 11 A 12 B 13 B 14 A 15 B

1 The building on the right is exactly half the height of the tallest building. This means the bottom line needs to be exactly halfway up the rectangle. This is only the case in B.

A is the view from the left side.

2 The main idea is that kangaroos are mainly left-handed. The rest of the text gives supporting information about what they use each hand for.

**B and D are incorrect.** This is supporting information for the main idea.

**C is incorrect.** This information is not in the text so cannot be the main idea.

3 According to the music teacher if a student has not practised for at least 50 hours, they do not have a chance of passing the exam. Therefore none of the students who have practised for less than 50 hours will pass the exam. So this statement must be true.

**A is incorrect.** According to the music teacher, practising for at least 50 hours gives a student only a **chance** of passing the exam. It does not guarantee a pass.

**C is incorrect.** The music teacher says students must have practised for **at least** 50 hours, not **less than** 50 hours.

**D is incorrect.** The music teacher says students **must** have practised for at least 50 hours so this statement cannot be true.

4 Using the same ideas as shown in the test skill pages, we can rotate the solids to try to fit them together.

Ask yourself where the sloped part will be when the solid is rotated. Focus on that bit and see if it will fit.

A method for rotating A is shown.

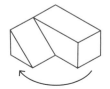

Rotate A.

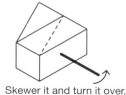

Skewer it and turn it over.

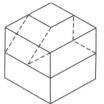

Place it on top of the original solid.

5 For Carter's conclusion to hold, it must be assumed that saving the wetlands is a good thing. (The wetlands are in danger + saving the wetlands is a good thing means therefore we must save the wetlands.)

**A is incorrect.** This is the conclusion Carter drew, based on the assumption that saving the wetlands is a good thing.

**B is incorrect.** The report from experts that the wetlands are in danger is the evidence Carter used to support his conclusion.

**D is incorrect.** This assumption would not support Carter's conclusion. (The wetlands are in danger + saving the wetlands is not necessary does not mean therefore we must save the wetlands.)

6 They can't get Vegetarian because Samantha doesn't like it. They can't get Supreme because Lincoln doesn't like it. So we only have Hawaiian and Cheese to choose from. Glen doesn't like Cheese so we are left with Hawaiian.

7 If David is telling the truth, then the money is his and everyone else is lying.

If Tanya is telling the truth, then the money is hers and everyone else is lying.

If the money is Roger's, then Mary is telling the truth and everyone else is lying.

But if the money is Mary's, then she and Roger are telling the truth and David and Tanya are lying.

8 Only Eli's reasoning is correct. We know that only students who attend the lunchtime meeting will be allowed to sing at the assembly. Since Eli will miss the meeting to go to the dentist he will not be allowed to sing.

**B is incorrect.** Although Lily will be attending the lunchtime meeting, there may be other reasons why some students are unable to sing at the assembly on Friday. So it is a flaw in her reasoning to say that she will **definitely** be singing.

**C and D are incorrect** by a process of elimination.

**9** The officer claims that boaters should wear a lifejacket at all times because wearing a lifejacket can save your life. The statement that seven out of ten people who drown while boating are not wearing a lifejacket best supports this claim.

**A is incorrect.** This statement gives further supporting information about lifejackets being important but does not support the claim about **wearing** the lifejacket to save your life.

**C is incorrect.** This statement is irrelevant to the claim.

**D is incorrect.** This statement might be the purpose of the interview but it is irrelevant to the officer's claim.

**10** Mint must be the smallest sector, so we can rule out B.

The strawberry sector must be twice as big as vanilla, so we can rule out C.

We are left with A and D. If we look carefully at A, we can see that the strawberry sector is a quarter circle. That means that vanilla must be half of that. We can see by looking at the line between the mint and vanilla sectors that this is not the case, as that line would make them the same size. We can rule out A. D is the answer.

**11** Bella has found a book that matches the description from her brother and assumes it **must** be the one he wants. However, it might not be the correct book because there may be other books with blue covers about goldfish.

**B is incorrect.** Bella says the book she found has a blue cover.

**C is incorrect.** Even if this is true, it is not a mistake Bella has made.

**D is incorrect.** Bella's brother said the book he wants is in the local library.

**12** The main idea is that it's important to take care of your teeth so this statement best expresses that. The rest of the text gives supporting information about how you can take care of your teeth.

**A and D are incorrect.** This is supporting information for the main idea.

**C is incorrect.** This information is not in the text so cannot be the main idea.

**13** Pamela lays a total of 4 + 4 + 5 = 13 eggs. Dawn lays a total of 3 + 6 + 5 = 14 eggs. Henrietta lays a total of 4 + 5 + 5 = 14 eggs. Velma lays a total of 6 + 2 + 3 = 11 eggs.

The two best layers are Dawn and Henrietta.

**14** If they do not give Archer's brother a laser tag voucher, you can conclude that they must give him a computer game. Since they give him a computer game, then they must also give him a book.

**B is incorrect.** You can conclude that Archer's brother will only get an electronic piggy bank if he doesn't get a book.

**C is incorrect.** Archer's brother will get a book or an electronic piggy bank, not both.

**D is incorrect.** Archer's mum says if they give Archer's brother a computer game, they will also give him a book.

**15** A, C and D fit as shown.

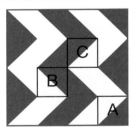

### SAMPLE TEST 1B

Page 27

1 D  2 D  3 C  4 D  5 B  6 C  7 B  8 C  9 B
10 A  11 C  12 A  13 B  14 B  15 A

**1** If Jamie scored more than Clair and Clair scored more than Rodney then the order must be Jamie, Clair, Rodney. As Moira scored less than Rodney she must have come 4th.

**2** Sofia's conclusion is that Jackson really likes vegemite. She has based this conclusion on the evidence that Jackson has had a vegemite sandwich for lunch for three days in a row. So for her conclusion to hold, it must be assumed Jackson would only have vegemite so often if he really liked vegemite. (Jackson has had a vegemite sandwich for lunch for three days in a row + Jackson would only have vegemite so often if he really liked vegemite means therefore Jackson really likes vegemite.) Jackson goes on to tell Sofia that he does not really like vegemite. So in this instance Sofia's assumption has led her to an incorrect conclusion.

**A is incorrect.** This is Sofia's conclusion, not her assumption.

**B is incorrect.** This is the real reason Jackson has vegemite for lunch but it is not the assumption Sofia has made and does not lead to the conclusion Sofia has come to.

**C is incorrect.** This is the evidence Sofia has used to base her conclusion on.

3   If Thomas is unlucky he will pick out all the blue and yellow shirts first. This is 6 shirts. After this there are only green shirts left, so the seventh shirt will definitely be green. This is the smallest number to be *certain* that he will get a green shirt.

4   Neither Willow nor Jun's reasoning is correct. Willow says it must be a leopard because it has spots but we are told that cheetahs also have spots. Therefore her reasoning is not correct when she says it **must** be a leopard. Jun says it cannot be a leopard because it isn't very large. We are told that leopards are larger than cheetahs. However, Jun could be looking at a young leopard so his reasoning is not correct when he says it **cannot** be a leopard.

**The other options are incorrect** by a process of elimination.

5   The busiest period must be when the most people are working. This must be between 10 am and 12 noon, when three people are working. Nino is not working during this period.

6   The square and the circle are in opposite corners. This rules out A and D. The flat side of the triangle and hexagon both face the circle. This rules out B. The answer is C.

7   The volunteer claims a fence is needed to protect nesting kookaburras because they have previously lost eggs to predators. The statement that kookaburra numbers are in decline

provides a reason why the kookaburra eggs need protection and therefore best supports this claim.

**A is incorrect.** This statement gives further supporting information about kookaburras but does not best support the claim that we must build a fence to support their eggs.

**C is incorrect.** This statement is irrelevant to the claim.

**D is incorrect.** This statement gives further supporting information about the area and protection of other species but does not best support the claim that we must build a fence to support their eggs.

8   C is a reflection of the piece at the top of the puzzle. It cannot be rotated to fit with the other three pieces to make a square.

9   B cannot be true because the volunteer nursery is not open on Tuesday afternoons.

**A is incorrect.** This conclusion could be true. The Garden is open during those times and, since Kala did not buy a plant, the nursery opening hours are irrelevant.

**C is incorrect.** This conclusion could be true. The Garden is open during those times and it is possible she did not buy a plant even though the volunteer nursery was also open.

**D is incorrect.** This conclusion could be true. The Garden and the volunteer nursery are open at that time.

10  If he makes one shoe in 15 minutes, he can make two shoes (or one pair) in 30 minutes.

Between 9 am and 5 pm there are 8 hours. Take half an hour out for lunch and the shoemaker works for 7 hours 30 minutes.

There are 15 lots of 30 minutes in 7 hours and 30 mins, as each hour is two lots of 30 minutes.

That means the shoemaker can make 15 pairs of shoes.

11  The main idea is that platypuses are monotremes. (Remember: The main idea is not necessarily at the beginning of a text.) The rest of the text gives supporting information about why platypuses are monotremes and about how few monotremes there are.

**A is incorrect.** This is supporting information for the main idea.

**B and D are incorrect.** This information is not in the text so cannot be the main idea.

**12** In each step, the number of sides of the first shape increases by one and the number of sides of the second shape decreases by one. So the first shape will have 5 + 1 = 6 sides, and the second shape will have 6 − 1 = 5 sides.

**13** Roses and lavender are both included in the list of plants Mum would like but neither Grandpa nor Aria mentions either one.

**A is incorrect.** Mum wants basil and roses but Aria would also like basil.

**C is incorrect.** Mum does not want passionfruit or thyme.

**D is incorrect.** Mum wants lavender and parsley but Aria would also like parsley

**14** If Edren chooses Modelling, she must choose it from List 3 as it is the only place it appears. Then she must choose Woodwork from List 2 as it cannot be chosen from List 3 and it doesn't appear in List 1. She must pick her third course from List 1. Cross-stitch is the only course in the options not available in List 1, so she cannot choose it.

**15** Talia's conclusion is that they won't hold a snake for a photo. She has based this conclusion on the evidence that George says it's scary to hold a snake. So for her conclusion to hold, it must be assumed that George does not want to be scared. (George says it's scary to hold a snake + George does not want to be scared means therefore they won't hold a snake for a photo.)

**B is incorrect.** This would not support Talia's conclusion that they won't hold a snake. George goes on to tell Talia that he does want to hold a snake. So, in this instance, Talia's assumption has led her to an incorrect conclusion.

**C is incorrect.** This is Talia's conclusion.

**D is incorrect.** This is the evidence Talia has used to draw her conclusion.

## SAMPLE TEST 2A Page 30

**1** A **2** B **3** C **4** D **5** B **6** B **7** B **8** D **9** C
**10** B **11** B **12** A **13** D **14** C **15** A

**1** The third building from the left is hidden by the second building when looking from the left. So there will only be two lines in the rectangle. This rules out C and D. The building on the left is half the height of the second building on the left so the lowest line will be at half the height of the second line. This rules out B. A is the answer.

**2** Harpo and Groucho say opposing things. They cannot both be telling the truth so one of them must be the liar. This means Chico must be telling the truth when he says that Harpo stole the cake.

**3** Livvy says she and Pudges are **sure** to move up a grade, whereas the trainer says completing the minimum tasks listed gives only a **chance** of moving up a grade.

**The other options are incorrect.** These statements do not show a mistake Livvy has made.

**4** Remy's father claims it's rude to use a mobile phone when you are with other people because it makes them feel less important. The statement that a study found even the presence of a mobile phone during a conversation made people feel less connected best supports this claim.

**A and C are incorrect.** These statements could weaken rather than support Remy's father's claim.

**B is incorrect.** This statement could support a claim that teenagers should limit their use of mobile phones but does not support the claim about their use being rude.

**5** Using the same ideas as shown in the test skill pages, we can rotate the solids to try to fit them together.

Ask yourself where the sloped part will be when the solid is rotated. Focus on that bit and see if it will fit.

The method shown below rotates the original solid to fit with B, shown here.

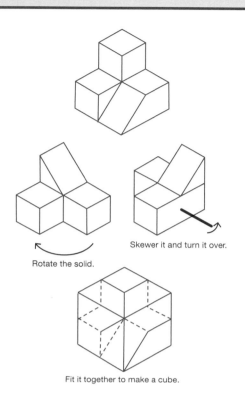

Rotate the solid.

Skewer it and turn it over.

Fit it together to make a cube.

**6** The developer claims the fun park, and the tourists it would bring, would support the local community on Crab Island. The statement that a fun park would destroy marine life which is important to the culture and way of life of the local community weakens this claim.

**A is incorrect.** This statement could support a claim that the fun park would support the local community.

**C is incorrect.** This statement neither supports nor weakens the claim about supporting the local community, although it could weaken a general argument about developing the island as a fun park.

**D is incorrect.** This statement could weaken a general argument about developing the island as a fun park but is not relevant to the claim about supporting the local community.

**7** They can't watch golf as Timo doesn't like it. They can't watch netball or swimming because Brenton doesn't like them. Patty watches everything except soccer. The only sport they all like is rugby league.

**8** The main idea the writer wants you to accept is that the ant is stronger than the elephant.

Remember that the main idea is not necessarily at the beginning of a text. The rest of the text gives supporting information about why the ant is stronger.

**A and B are incorrect.** This is supporting information for the main idea.

**C is incorrect.** This information is not in the text so cannot be the main idea.

**9** According to the organiser if an entrant does not clear at least ten obstacles, they do not have a chance of getting a prize. Therefore none of the students who clear less than ten obstacles will win a prize. So C must be true.

**A is incorrect.** According to the organiser, clearing ten obstacles gives an entrant only a **chance** of winning a prize. It does not guarantee a prize.

**B is incorrect.** The organiser says entrants must clear **at least** ten obstacles, not **less than** ten obstacles.

**D is incorrect.** The organiser says entrants **must** clear at least ten obstacles to win a prize so this statement cannot be true.

**10** If 6 more people liked lions than panthers, then the three extra rectangles represent 6 people. That means each rectangle represents 2 people, as $6 \div 3 = 2$.

All up there are 16 rectangles, each representing 2 people. $16 \times 2 = 32$ people.

**11** For Ari's conclusion to hold, it must be assumed they should not make their mother angry. (Their mum will be angry if they are not home by five o'clock + they should not make their mother angry means therefore they should hurry home.)

**A is incorrect.** This is the conclusion Ari has drawn, based on the assumption that they should not make their mother angry.

**C is incorrect.** This is the evidence Ari has used to support his conclusion.

**D is incorrect.** This assumption would not support Ari's conclusion. (Their mum will be angry if they are not home by five o'clock + it doesn't matter if their mum gets angry does not mean therefore they should hurry home.)

**12** Only Poppy's reasoning is correct. We know that whenever Poppy's neighbour's team wins it puts him in a good mood. And when he is in a good mood, he **always** plays his music loudly.

**B is incorrect.** Kamal has not thought there might be other reasons why Poppy's neighbour is in a good mood and so is playing music loudly. He has also failed to consider there might be other reasons why he is playing music loudly.

**C and D are incorrect** by a process of elimination.

**13** A, B and C fit as shown.

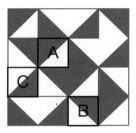

**14** The scientist claims that plantations with a single species of tree are not a solution for climate change and might actually do more harm because plantations do not store carbon in the same way that mixed forests do. The statement that studies have shown single-species plantations emit more carbon than they absorb best supports this claim.

**A is incorrect.** This statement provides extra supporting information about the differences between single-species and mixed old-growth forests but does not best support the claim that single-species plantations are not a solution for climate change.

**B is incorrect.** This statement provides extra supporting information about mixed old-growth forests but on its own does not best support the claim that single-species plantations are not a solution for climate change.

**D is incorrect.** This statement does not support the claim that single-species plantations are not a solution for climate change.

**15** The first thing we need to find out is how many eggs are left to find between Dante and Parvati. The other three friends have found 1 + 5 + 2 = 8 eggs which means there are 20 − 8 = 12 eggs left to be found.

We can see that Dante is 5 behind Parvati as he is on 2 and she is on 7 after the backyard. This means he need to beat her by six in the front yard to be ahead by 1 egg after both yards.

We need to find a pair of numbers that adds to 12 with 6 between them. Our numbers are 9 and 3.

If Dante finds 9 eggs and Parvati finds the other 3, then Dante will have 11 eggs and Parvati will have 10 eggs. He will beat her by one egg.

## SAMPLE TEST 2B

Page 34

**1** B **2** A **3** D **4** C **5** C **6** A **7** D **8** B **9** C
**10** C **11** C **12** D **13** D **14** D **15** D

**1** We do not know which seat each person is sitting in but we know how they are spread around the table. One possible arrangement is shown.

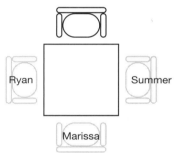

If Ryan and Summer are both next to Marissa, then she must be seated between them, opposite the empty chair. Ryan might be on her right but could also be on her left, as shown.

**2** A is not possible because the instant download was only available online and Bodhi would only get reward points if he purchased the game at the game store, not online.

**B and C are incorrect.** These are possible if he buys the game from the game store.

**D is incorrect.** This is possible if he buys the game online.

**3** If Colin is unlucky, he will pick out all the green and red lollies first. This is 9 lollies. Once this has happened, the 10th lolly he takes from the bag will be a white lolly.

**4** The main idea the writer wants you to accept is to wear a helmet when you ride a bike. The rest of the text gives supporting information about why you should wear a helmet.

**A and D are incorrect.** This is supporting information for the main idea.

**B is incorrect.** This information is not in the text so cannot be the main idea.

**5** Pottery and Drawing are both available on Friday but neither is available on Tuesday. Peta can only choose one of these classes.

**6** The small square and the triangle are in opposite corners. This rules out C. The pointy bit of the hexagon is aiming at the pointy bit of the triangle. This rules out D and B. The answer is A.

**7** If Mimi does not debate, you can conclude that Zoe must make it to the debate. Since Zoe makes it, Isaac must also be on the team.

**A is incorrect.** The club captain says Isaac or David will debate, not both.

**B is incorrect.** The club captain says if Zoe can make it, Isaac will also be on the team.

**C is incorrect.** We know that since Mimi does not debate, Zoe must make it. Therefore Isaac must be on the team instead of David.

**8** In A, the piece on the left is reflected and the piece on the right is not correct. In C, the piece on the left is not correct, as it has an extra side. In D, the piece on the right is a reflection of the correct piece.

**9** For the sign's conclusion to hold, it must be assumed that the kittens will sell out quickly. (The kittens are adorable and instore now + the kittens will sell out quickly means therefore get in quickly if you want to buy one.)

**A is incorrect.** This is the sign's conclusion.

**B is incorrect.** This is the evidence for the sign's conclusion.

**D is incorrect.** This is the purpose of the sign, not its assumption. (The kittens are adorable and instore now + the pet store wants to sell all the kittens does not mean therefore get in quickly if you want to buy one.)

**10** If Colleen washes 3 dogs per hour it takes her 20 minutes to wash one dog. So she washes 6 dogs between 8 am and 10 am plus two more dogs. This takes her to 8 dogs.

$$8 \times \$10 = \$80$$

**11** Both Josh and Mila are correct. Josh is correct because we are told that if the mum buys a new dress, it's **always** because there is a sale on. Mila is correct because we are told the mum only buys a dress when there is a sale on, not that she **always** buys a dress whenever there is a sale. So it is correct to reason there could be a sale even though their mum has not bought a dress.

**The other options are incorrect** by a process of elimination.

**12** In each step, both lightning bolts makes a quarter turn in the anticlockwise direction and the purple shifts from left to right and back again. Following this pattern, the lightning bolt on the left will be white and pointing to the left, while the bolt on the right will be purple and pointing down. The answer is D.

**13** The ad claims we should maintain our smoke alarms to make sure they work in case there is a fire. The statement that the Fire and Rescue Department recommends smoke alarms should be vacuum cleaned every six months best supports this claim about the need for maintenance.

**A and B are incorrect.** These statements are not relevant to the claim about the need for maintenance.

**C is incorrect.** This statement could be why the company has made the ad but does not support the claim about the need for maintenance.

**14** S E E   Y O U   A T   S C H O O L
E S Y   E U O   T A   C S O H L O

**15** Oscar has concluded that some of the teachers must have walked because he knows eleven teachers drive to school and he only saw eight cars in the car park. Therefore he must think that teachers always either drive or walk to school. He has not considered that there are other ways for the teachers to get to school or that some teachers might not be at school on this particular day.

**The other options are incorrect.** These statements do not show a mistake Oscar has made.

## SAMPLE TEST 3A

Page 38

1 D  2 B  3 C  4 D  5 B  6 C  7 A  8 B  9 C
10 A  11 C  12 B  13 B  14 A  15 D

1   When looking from the right we will be able to see three balls. The two smallest balls will be hidden. This rules out A and C. We can see that the ball on the right is taller than the first line. This rules out B. The answer is D.

2   Michaela reasons correctly when she predicts that if Ollie's mother lets Ollie's brother choose a treat this Friday, he must have earned ten stars.

    **A is incorrect.** Jenna uses incorrect reasoning to claim that because Ollie says his brother got a treat last Friday, his little brother must have got all his spelling words correct. The star chart is for good behaviour and not just spelling. Ollie's brother might have earned ten stars through behaviour other than results in the spelling test.

    **C and D are incorrect** by a process of elimination.

3   Johanna has postcards from Spain and Indonesia which neither Billy nor Taylah has.

4   Using the same ideas as shown in the test skill pages, we can rotate the solids to try to fit them together.

    Ask yourself where the sloped part will be when the solid is rotated. Focus on that bit and see if it will fit.

    A method for rotating D so it fits together with the original solid is shown.

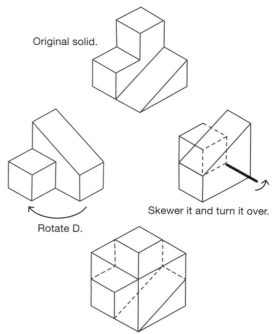

Original solid.

Rotate D.

Skewer it and turn it over.

Fit them together to make a cube.

5   The information tells you it is not possible for Harriet to improve her goal shooting if she only practises on Tuesdays for 90 minutes. You are told she needs to practise at least three times a week for an hour each time.

    **The other answers are incorrect.** These statements cannot be true.

6   Cormoran doesn't like rock climbing, Midge doesn't like bushwalking and Charlotte doesn't like surfing. This leaves waterskiing and snowboarding but Robyn only likes snowboarding out of those two, so it must be the answer.

7   Declan and Maurice say opposite things so one of them must be telling the truth and the other must be lying.

    As only one of the four people is telling the truth, Bella and Kevin must also be lying. Bella is lying when she says that Kevin didn't do it. Therefore Kevin left the gate open.

8   The argument the text's creator wants you to accept is that urgent action is needed to save the Southern Corroboree frog from extinction. Reasons given to support the argument include the fact that the frogs form a critical part of the ecosystem. The text also includes information about what is being done to save the frog.

**A is incorrect.** This statement adds new information about why the frogs are endangered so cannot be the main idea expressed in the text.

**C is incorrect.** This statement paraphrases information in the text about the program to save the frogs.

**D is incorrect.** This is a statement of fact in the text but not the main idea.

9   The argument is that mud bricks are a superior housing material to concrete bricks. The statement which weakens the argument is the fact that mud-brick homes need to be built on waterproof foundations—the implication being that mud bricks are not waterproof.

**A is incorrect.** It strengthens the argument.

**B and D are incorrect.** They neither strengthen nor weaken the argument.

10  Company 4 increased their sales the most, so this must be Qizz. Company 3 sold the most over the two years so this must be Woop. Companies 1 and 4 made the same combined total so Company 1 must be Zing. Blinx must be Company 2.

11  Suzuka uses incorrect reasoning. She cannot claim that because the marsupial has short legs it must be a wallaby. It could be a young kangaroo or a different kind of marsupial. She can only reasonably claim that it **might** be a wallaby.

Madison uses incorrect reasoning. She cannot claim the animal is a kangaroo because it is over a metre tall. The information tells you that wallabies rarely grow more than one metre tall, not that they never grow more than one metre tall. The animal is not likely to be a wallaby. However, it **could** be a wallaby so Madison is incorrect.

12  Scarlet has found a pair of shoes that are her own size but she cannot assume they are Sana's just because Sana is the same age and height as her.

**A is incorrect.** This statement doesn't make sense. Sana has told Toby that the shoes are normal black lace-ups.

**C is incorrect.** This sentence could be true but is not the mistake Scarlet has made.

**D is incorrect.** This sentence doesn't make sense. Toby is looking for Sana's shoes so it isn't true that he might not want to collect them. Also this is not the mistake Scarlet has made.

13  The total time for each sprinter is shown.

Matt has a combined total of $11.0 + 20.0 = 31.0$ seconds.

Rohan has a combined total of $10.1 + 20.2 = 30.3$ seconds.

Jesse has a combined total of $10.5 + 19.9 = 30.4$ seconds.

Carl has a combined total of $9.9 + 21.0 = 30.9$ seconds.

Rohan's is the smallest total. He is the best sprinter.

14  If Yuta is not playing then Dante must be playing. Since Dante will be playing, then Meghan must also be playing but not William.

**The other options are incorrect** by a process of elimination.

15  A, B and C fit as shown below.

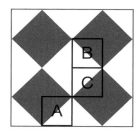

## SAMPLE TEST 3B Page 42

1 C  2 D  3 C  4 D  5 B  6 C  7 C  8 D  9 A
10 C  11 C  12 D  13 D  14 A  15 B

1   Nico finished before Fernando and Fernando finished before Daniel and Sergio. So Nico must have finished first and Fernando finished second.

**2** The creator of the argument wants you to accept that some people do not like the taste of broccoli due to their genes. The statement that cheese or soy sauce masks the flavour of broccoli means that people can eat broccoli without really tasting it. This weakens the argument.

**The other options are incorrect.** They might be true but do not weaken the argument that some people have a genetic reason for not being able to eat broccoli.

**3** There are 20 cards in total and, divided by 4, that means each friend receives 5 cards. It is possible that one friend will receive 5 black cards and no red cards, so the answer is not D. If this happens, the other black card will go to someone that has four red cards and the other two friends will have 5 red cards each. So three friends must have at least 1 red card.

**4** Samir often uses tarragon and dill, which neither Daivik nor Amelia uses.

**The other options are incorrect** by a process of elimination.

**5** The large square and the hexagon are in opposite corners. This rules out A and C. The pointy bit of the hexagon and the pointy bit of the small square are aiming at each other. This rules out D. The answer is B.

**6** If she goes shopping from 10 am – 12 noon Rugs Galore will be closed.

If she goes from 12 noon – 2 pm Tables 'r' Us will be closed.

If she goes from 4 pm – 6 pm Computers Co will be closed.

Each store is open for at least 1 hour between 2 pm and 4 pm.

**7** The argument that the creator of the text wants you to accept is that Nolan's series of paintings about Ned Kelly are amazing and worth taking the time to view if you can. The statement which adds to the argument is that the story of Ned Kelly makes an interesting topic for a series of artworks.

**A is incorrect.** This statement is in the text already so cannot strengthen it.

**B and D are incorrect.** These statements add further detail to the subject; they do not strengthen the claim made in the text.

**8** In A, the piece on the bottom left is a reflection of the required piece. In B, the piece on the right is not correct, as it has fewer sides. In C, the piece at the top is not wide enough.

**9** If there are plenty of great pop stars who don't dance, then Stevie cannot claim that to become a pop star you have to be a great dancer as well as a great singer. This sentence shows the mistake Stevie has made.

**B is incorrect.** This sentence is about popular songs rather than pop stars.

**C and D are incorrect.** They might be true but are not the mistake Stevie has made.

**10** Before lunch, Glenda works for 5 hours as 7:00 am – 12:00 noon is 5 hours. After lunch, Glenda works for 2 hours and 30 minutes, as lunch finishes at 12:30 pm and she works until 3:00 pm. The difference between the two time periods is 5:00 – 2:30 = 2:30 (remember that 30 minutes is half an hour) or 5 – 2.5 = 2.5. So we need to work out how many bricks she lays in 2 hours 30 minutes (2.5 hours).

120 bricks / h × 2.5 hours = 300 bricks

**11** Both children use correct reasoning. Ashley says she can hear the baby crying so it is correct to reason that they should check on her. Novak is correct in recommending that they need to do as his mother asked and wait before going in because he cannot hear the baby crying.

**The other options are incorrect** by a process of elimination.

**12** In Step 2 the crescent makes a quarter turn in an anticlockwise direction. In Step 3 the arrow makes a quarter turn in the clockwise direction. In Step 4 the crescent makes another quarter turn in an anticlockwise direction. So after this the arrow must make a quarter turn in the clockwise direction. The answer is D.

**13** The statement that a minimum two hours of assembly is required might limit Isobel's ability to sell the cubby house. Some people might not be in a position to assemble the cubby themselves.

**A and B are incorrect.** They strengthen rather than weaken Isobel's ability to sell the cubby house.

**C is incorrect.** It does not weaken the argument because children under the age of one are too young to play in a cubby house.

**14** If more than half of the students picked blue or red, they make up more than half the circle. In D, they make up exactly half the circle so D is not correct. If more than a quarter picked red or yellow, they make up more than a quarter of the circle. In B they make up exactly a quarter of the circle, so B is not correct. The same goes for green and yellow. In C they make up exactly a quarter, so C is not correct. The answer is A.

**15** B is the only option possible. If Gretchen does not attend then you know that Dom will be invited and not Marcus. Because Gretchen is not attending, Kanami will invite Will and not Marcus. (The information states that if Gretchen does attend, then Marcus will be invited and not Will.) So you know that because Gretchen is not attending, Will and Dom will be invited.

**C and D are incorrect** because Marcus will not be invited.

**A is incorrect.** Gretchen is not allowed to attend.

## SAMPLE TEST 4A

Page 46

1 B  2 C  3 A  4 C  5 A  6 B  7 B  8 B  9 A
10 C  11 A  12 C  13 D  14 B  15 A

**1** From the left, the top of the first ball lies between the first two height lines. This rules out A and C. The next ball we see is three lines high and the largest is four. This rules out D. The answer is B.

**2** C cannot be true because the bowling alley is not open on a Monday.

**A is incorrect.** This sentence could be true. The bowling alley opens at 10 am on a Wednesday.

**B is incorrect.** This sentence could be true. The bowling alley opens from 10 am to 6 pm on Thursdays.

**D is incorrect** This sentence could be true. The bowling alley is open until 6 pm on a Sunday.

**3** Uncle Jim's mistake is that he cannot conclude that Aunty Denise will definitely have the pavlova made in three hours when Aunty Denise says she needs to start baking by 9 am **at the latest** to have any chance of getting the pavlova made by 12. This means it's possible, not certain, that she'll have it made in time.

**B is incorrect.** This is Uncle Jim's assumption and not what Denise has said.

**C is incorrect.** This is not the mistake Uncle Jim has made regarding the pavlova being ready in time.

**D is incorrect.** This is irrelevant to Uncle Jim's error in reasoning.

**4** Using the same ideas as shown in the test skill pages, we can rotate the solids to try to fit them together.

Ask yourself where the sloped part will be when the solid is rotated. Focus on that bit and see if it will fit.

A method for rotating C so it fits together with the original solid is shown.

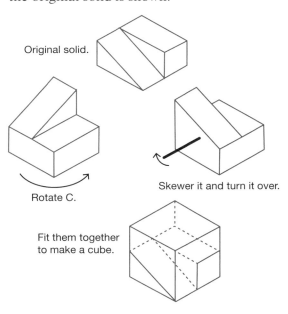

Original solid.

Rotate C.

Skewer it and turn it over.

Fit them together to make a cube.

**5**   The argument that eating carrots will maintain eye health is undermined by the statement that some eye diseases cannot be prevented by eating carrots. It can be inferred that many of these diseases will have a negative effect on eyesight.

**B is incorrect.** This statement adds to the claim that carrots are healthy for eyes and adds other activities that support eye health.

**C and D are incorrect.** These statements are irrelevant to the argument.

**6**   Brad doesn't like grapefruit, so it can't be A. Rachel only likes grapefruit, peaches and cherries, so it can't be D. Micaela only likes grapefruit, mangoes and peaches so it can't be C. The answer is B.

**7**   Peter says Katy did it but Katy says she didn't. So only one of them can be telling the truth and the other must be lying.

As only one of the four children is a liar, Charles and Rocco are both telling the truth. Charles is telling the truth when he says that Peter spilled the paint.

**8**   The main idea is that Swiss people love their cats and erect ramps and cat ladders to give their cats freedom of movement.

**A is incorrect.** This is a fact in the text but not the main idea.

**C is incorrect.** This is true in the text but does not take account of the fact that cat owners erect the ladders because they love their cats.

**D is incorrect.** This is true in the text but does not take account of how much Swiss people love their cats.

**9**   Yassi uses incorrect reasoning. He says to make sure the fabric is **not** non-flammable. He should have said to make sure the fabric **is** non-flammable as that means it does not readily catch on fire.

**B is incorrect.** Rhiannon uses correct reasoning to recommend that children stay away from heaters, candles and open fires regardless of whether their clothing is highly flammable or not.

**The other options are incorrect** by a process of elimination.

**10**   The difference between Cooper's best and worst marks is the largest. Person 2 scored 10 in Week 2 and 4 in Week 4. $10 - 4 = 6$ which is larger than the differences for the other students. Cooper must be Person 2.

Kyle was the only student to get the same mark in two tests. Person 1 scored 6 in both Week 2 and Week 4. Kyle must be Person 1.

This means Maddie is Person 3 and she scored 7 and 9 in her last two tests. $7 + 9 = 16$

The answer is C.

**11**   The argument is that a meat-free diet is better for the planet because it saves on methane emissions and water use. This statement strengthens the argument by giving an additional reason why meat-free eating is better for the planet.

**The other options are incorrect.** These options support the school's stand on having a meat-free canteen but do not strengthen the argument about why being meat-free is good for the planet.

**12**   Marco has concluded that Kaliah's mum's new friend must be vegan. To draw this conclusion he used the evidence that Kaliah's mum is going to make a vegan Thai red curry with rice for dinner. His assumption must therefore be that Kahliah's mum will cook vegan food only if the guest is vegan.

**The other options are incorrect.** These statements do not lead to Marco's conclusion that the guest must be vegan.

**13**   To find out who is in the lead we need to find the total number of shots played after both rounds. The player with the smallest total is in the lead.

Ernie is on $75 + 62 = 137$.
Minjee is on $63 + 72 = 135$.
Rory is on $68 + 68 = 136$.
Babe is on $70 + 64 = 134$.

Babe is in the lead after the second round.

**14**   This option is not possible. The after-hours clinic opens at 6 pm but does not take appointments.

**The other options are incorrect.** They are all possible.

**15** If Helen finishes after Dawn but before Pamela then Dawn must have finished before both of them. If Dawn also finishes before Trish, then she beats everyone and must have come first. She cannot have come second.

## SAMPLE TEST 4B

Page 50

1 D  2 D  3 A  4 C  5 B  6 D  7 B  8 D  9 A
10 C  11 C  12 D  13 C  14 B  15 C

**1** We do not know which seat each person is sitting in but we know how they are spread around the table. One possible arrangement is shown.

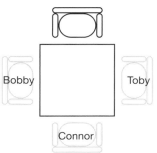

Bobby   Toby

Connor

If Toby and Bobby are sitting opposite each other then, wherever Connor sits, he is sitting next to Bobby. Toby might be on Connor's left, but he might be on his right, as shown.

**2** The main idea in the text is that the Superb lyrebird does a great job helping the environment. The rest of the text supports this main idea. The fact that the lyrebird aerates the soil, spreads leaf litter and makes grooves and channels in the soil for other species to use supports the main idea.

**A and B are incorrect.** These statements support the main idea.

**C is incorrect.** This is a description so is not the main idea of the text.

**3** If five pizzas are bought, then there are 20 slices of pizza to be shared.

If every person receives 3 slices of pizza, then there will need to be 21 slices of pizza as $7 \times 3 = 21$. So 6 people will get 3 slices and one person will get 2 slices. This rules out B, C and D as solutions.

Also, there are 8 slices of Vegetarian. Once everyone has received 1 slice of Vegetarian, there is 1 slice left. This must be given out, and so will be given to someone who already has a piece of Vegetarian. So someone will get 2 slices of the same type of pizza.

**4** Neither Flynn nor Aaron chooses the salad or garlic bread at the buffet.

**The other options are incorrect** by a process of elimination.

**5** The friends can all eat at together at 10 am, 5 pm and 7 pm. So they can eat breakfast, tea and dinner together but they cannot all eat lunch together.

**6** A is the view from Goanna Road. B is the view from Koala Avenue. C is the view from Penguin Parade. D is **not** the view from Platypus Drive.

**7** Emily uses correct reasoning. If Jaffa is left outside tomorrow and barks all day, then the nurse will not get any sleep and will be upset.

**A is incorrect.** Philippe uses incorrect reasoning when he asserts that because Yi Min's neighbour, the nurse, was upset on Tuesday night, Jaffa must have been left outside to bark all day Tuesday. The information in the box tells you the nurse gets upset when she can't get enough sleep so she might have been upset with Jaffa's barking. However, there may have been other reasons she missed out on sleep and got upset.

**C and D are incorrect** by a process of elimination.

**8** The three pieces go together as shown below. None of the other options work.

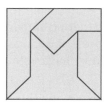

**9** Dane has made a mistake in asserting that the herb must be coriander just because it has a green leaf and has a strong smell. The text tells you coriander has a stronger smell than parsley but Dane does not seem to have compared the herb he's chosen with any other herb. In addition, just because it has a green leaf does not mean it is necessarily coriander.

**B and C are incorrect.** These are statements in the text and not the mistake Dane has made. **D is incorrect.** It seems likely that Dane rubbed the leaves of the herb he thinks is coriander between his fingers, as instructed by Sasha's mum, but it seems he hasn't compared the aroma with any other herb.

10 Each square metre requires 4 pavers and Ian can lay 16 pavers in an hour. This means he can lay 4 square metres in an hour as $4 × 4 = 16$.

It will take Ian 5 hours to lay tiles over the 20 square metres as $20 ÷ 4 = 5$.

5 hours after 7:30 am is 12:30 pm.

11 Neither Young-ro nor Louis cooks parsnips or capsicum in their air fryers.

12 The main idea is expressed in the final sentence of the text. The rest of the information provides examples to support the main idea. The first sentence introduces the idea of families having special words that they use together. The body of the text provides examples of the special words used by Jamal's family members. The final sentence sums up the text and is the main idea.

13 The arrow is being rotated by 45 degrees in an anticlockwise direction each step. The next step will show an arrow pointing upwards.

14 The message is written using cipher 2. This means the first letter of the message is B not C. The second letter is R not S and the third letter is I not J. The message starts BRI... Knowing that can you work out what the message says?

15 Since everyone had to vote for two of the topics, knowing that no student voted for both Tropical Rainforest and Under the Sea tells you every student must have voted for Desert Habitat.

**A is incorrect.** Knowing this allows you to narrow the vote to these two topics but it doesn't allow you to know the winner.

**B is incorrect.** Knowing this allows you to narrow the vote to Tropical Rainforest and one of the other two but does not allow you to know the result.

**D is incorrect.** This tells you that Under the Sea did not win but does not allow you to know the result of the vote.

## SAMPLE TEST 5A
Page 54

1 C  2 A  3 B  4 D  5 B  6 C  7 B  8 C  9 D
10 C  11 C  12 D  13 A  14 C  15 B

1 If we looked at C from the side, there would be a vertical line in either the first or second level to show the corner of one of the square prisms.

2 Bryan has concluded that Sheridan must love quinoa. Bryan's evidence is that Sheridan claims to have found a great new recipe using quinoa. To have found a recipe implies Sheridan had been looking for a recipe. Bryan's assumption must be that Sheridan has searched for a quinoa recipe. He has assumed people search for recipes that use ingredients they love.

**The other answers are incorrect.** They do not lead to Bryan's conclusion.

3 Monique uses correct reasoning to state that she **doubts** Bindi will win *Best in Breed*.

**A is incorrect.** Kashif uses incorrect reasoning to declare that Eric's dog is sure to win the *Best in Breed* category again this year. He cannot be sure of the outcome of the competition.

**C and D are incorrect** by a process of elimination.

4 The solutions for A, B and C are shown below. The pieces in D do not fit together to make the solid.

5 The argument is that when you donate to a charity some of the money is used for the charity's administration costs and is considered wasted. Any argument that allays fears about wasted administration costs will weaken the argument. The claim that running a charity

costs money and these costs are not a waste of money weakens Anastasia's stepdad's argument because it reassures people that the charity is not wasting money.

**A and D are incorrect.** These statements are irrelevant to the argument.

**C is incorrect.** This statement supports, rather than weakens, the argument.

6  Tree 1 produced $40 + 35 + 40 + 50 = 165$ kg.
Tree 2 produced $60 + 20 + 45 + 35 = 160$ kg.
Tree 3 produced $30 + 25 + 50 + 35 = 140$ kg.

So Tree 1 is the lemon tree as it produced the most fruit. Tree 2 is the orange tree as $60 + 20 = 80$ and $45 + 35 = 80$ which means the amount of fruit it produced was the same in both the first two years and the second two years. Tree 3 must be the grapefruit tree. In its second-best year it produced 35 kg.

7  Geri only likes birds, rabbits and cats so it must be one of these animals. Ray doesn't like rabbits and Patrick doesn't like birds so the family should get a cat.

8  The teacher said that to have even a chance of learning their lines perfectly by the time they have to perform for an audience, students who are main characters must have at least fifteen hours of practice. So none of the main character actors who have had less than fifteen hours of practice will have learnt their lines in time.

**A, B and D are incorrect.** These statements cannot be true as they do not make sense.

9  The main idea in the text is that feeding birds human food has negative consequences for their health. The text explains that birds need their natural diet and describes what the negative consequences are of feeding birds human food such as bread and raw meat.

10  If there were three times as many pigeons as king parrots, then species 2, which is one rectangle, is the king parrot and species 3, 3 rectangles, is the pigeon.

There are more galahs than rosellas so species 1 must be the rosella and species 4 the galah. The galah has 2 more rectangles than the rosella and these rectangles represent 6 birds. Each rectangle represents 3 birds.

There are 5 rectangles for the rosella and 5 lots of 3 birds is 15 birds.

11  Both Joshua and Christina use correct reasoning. Joshua uses correct reasoning to suggest that even though sloths sleep in the treetops, his mum probably doesn't call Uncle Doug a sloth for that reason. Christina correctly reasons that because a sloth is lethargic and slow moving, Joshua's mum probably thinks Uncle Doug is lazy or sleepy.

12  Neither Tallulah nor Lai has been to Lismore or Dorrigo. Keeley has.

**The other answers are incorrect** by a process of elimination.

13  Ruby slept for a total of $13 + 10 = 23$ hours. Theo slept for 31 hours and Delilah for 33 hours. For Pepe to be the laziest cat he must have slept for more than 33 hours. As $33 - 16 = 17$ Pepe must have slept for more than 17 hours. If he had slept for 17 hours exactly, he would have been equally as lazy as Delilah.

It might be true that Pepe slept for more than 18 hours. It might be true that Pepe slept more than Theo. It might be true that Pepe slept for less than 20 hours. But it is not certain.

14  Suhana has used the evidence that Tristan is planting a lemon tree and expects to grow lots of lemons to conclude that Tristan must eat a lot of lemons. Suhana's assumption must be that anyone who chooses to grow lemons must like to eat lemons. Remember that assumptions may not be correct. Tristan might have other reasons to grow lemons.

**A is incorrect.** This could not be true because not everyone grows lemons and also it is not the assumption Sahana has made.

**B and D are incorrect.** These sentences are not assumptions Sahana has made.

15  If John is given the second-largest jumper and Hannah is not given the smallest jumper then either William or Kristine is given the smallest jumper. But we know Kristine's jumper is smaller than William's so she must have the smallest jumper, which is yellow.

## SAMPLE TEST 5B    Page 58

1 B  2 A  3 A  4 B  5 A  6 C  7 B  8 D  9 A
10 A  11 C  12 C  13 D  14 A  15 D

1   If Nicola is sitting opposite Cora, then Cora cannot be sitting opposite Fleur. B is impossible. Fleur must be sitting opposite the empty chair and might be on Cora's left or her right.

2   The creator of the text wants you to accept the argument that malaria can be deadly but is easily preventable. The text provides two ways to prevent the spread of malaria. This option provides a third way so it is the option that best supports the argument.

   **B is incorrect.** This statement is about treatment rather than prevention.

   **C is incorrect.** This statement is about symptoms rather than prevention.

   **D is incorrect.** This is an additional statement of fact about malaria but does not support the argument.

3   If Jericho is unlucky, he will draw all of the black and blue marbles first. This is 7 marbles. Now there are only yellow marbles left in the bag. The next two marbles he draws will be yellow. So after 9 marbles are drawn he must have at least 2 yellow marbles.

4   Ms Peacock assumes that, because there are only five photos of dogs on the back wall, three students who own dogs must have forgotten to bring their photos. Her mistake is that she has assumed each child who has a dog would choose to bring a photo of the dog and not one of their other pets.

   **A is incorrect.** This could be true but is not the mistake Ms Peacock made when she declared three children had forgotten their photos.

   **C is incorrect.** Ms Peacock knows eight children own dogs.

   **D is incorrect.** This is a mistake but not the mistake made by Ms Peacock when she declared that three children forgot their photos.

5   B is the view from Howard Parade. C is the view from Whitlam Road. D is the view from Fraser Street. But A is **not** the view from Hawke Highway.

6   Kris said she didn't eat the spaghetti but Lily said she did. One of these two must be the liar, which means Yusuf is telling the truth when he says that Lily ate the spaghetti.

7   The argument is that lightning strikes can kill or injure a person and the advice is to avoid behaviour that puts you at risk of being struck by lightning. The rest of the text gives supporting information to tell where and how people die and in which area of Australia there are the most lightning strikes.

8   The solutions for the other options are shown below. There is no way to use the pieces given to create the picture shown in D.

9   Nasin uses the evidence that Charlie practises a lot to conclude that Charlie must be hopeless (to need so much practice). Nasin's assumption must be that only people who are hopeless practise as much as Charlie.

   **The other answers are incorrect.** None of them lead to Nasin's conclusion.

10  The arrow is rotating by 45 degrees in the clockwise direction each turn. The arrow missing should be pointing straight down.

11  The vet claims the cat is overweight, which is bad for its health, and suggests ways to help the cat lose weight. Any statement that contributes further information about the problems of being overweight or provides weight-loss tips will support the vet's claim. The statement that being overweight can lead to diseases such as diabetes best supports the vet's claims.

   **The other options are incorrect.** They might be true but do not support the vet's claims.

**12** Carlos delivers 40 menus in one hour which means he delivers 20 menus in half an hour (30 minutes) and 10 menus in a quarter of an hour (15 minutes). He works for 3 hours and 15 minutes all up after his break is taken into account.

$$3 \text{ hours} \times 40 \text{ menus / h} = 120 \text{ menus}$$

And then we add the 10 menus he delivers in 15 minutes.

$$120 + 10 = 130 \text{ menus}$$

**13** Paris has concluded that Cassie does not care if her car is dirty, based on the evidence that Cassie never washes her car. Paris must have made the assumption that if Cassie cared about her car being dirty, she'd wash it. This assumption may not be true. There are many reasons why Cassie may have a dirty car. For example, she may not have had time to wash it herself or the money to pay for it to be washed. She may be physically unable to wash it herself. Note that incorrect assumptions can lead to incorrect conclusions, i.e. Cassie may in fact care that her car is dirty.

**The other options are incorrect.** They could be true but are not assumptions made by Paris.

**14** The best way to attack these questions is to quickly write out the alphabet, making sure that you have all 26 letters. You can then count back three letters as you go along. In A, you will get PUDDHMF, a misspelling of PUDDING because Malcolm only counted back by two letters for the ING instead of by three letters. Can you work out what the other words say?

**15** It cannot be true that native bees are the most common bees in Australia because the text tells you the European honey bee is the most common bee in Australia.

**A is incorrect.** It is true that introduced bees and native bees eat the same food. You are told they compete for food.

**B is incorrect.** It must be true that early colonists enjoyed honey because the text tells you the European honey bee was introduced to Australia in 1822 by the early colonists to make honey.

**C is incorrect.** You can conclude that introduced species of bee are a threat to native bees and native plants because they compete with native bees for food and nesting sites. Also they don't pollinate some of the native flowers and those plants could become endangered.

# NOTES

# NOTES

# NOTES